DATE DUE

1 4 1969

W9-AUG-728

THE BOOM
IN GOING BUST

THE BOOM
IN GOING BUST

The threat of a
national scandal
in consumer bankruptcy

BY

GEORGE SULLIVAN

The Macmillan Company, *New York*

Collier-Macmillan Limited, *London*

Copyright © 1968 by George Sullivan

All rights reserved. No part of this book may be reproduced or transmitted in any form or by any means, electronic or mechanical, including photocopying, recording or by any information storage and retrieval system, without permission in writing from the Publisher.

Library of Congress Catalog Card Number: 68–25716

FIRST PRINTING

The Macmillan Company, New York
Collier-Macmillan Canada Ltd., Toronto, Ontario

Printed in the United States of America

HG
3766
S78

Ha 29A968

CONTENTS

INTRODUCTION

Our culture is rich in Horatio Alger tales, but very little has been written about fortunes that go the other way—from riches to rags—a fact the Brookings Institution noted recently. This may be why literature on the subject of individual or personal (not business) bankruptcy—aside from technical reports prepared by sociologists, economists or government officials, and material meant especially for bankruptcy lawyers—is practically non-existent.

The Superintendent of Documents of the Government Printing Office in Washington publishes books and pamphlets on *every* subject, but on the subject of bankruptcy all that is available is a thick book entitled *Bankruptcy Laws of the United States*. It costs $1. It is 375 pages of the most laborious reading one can imagine.

Bankruptcy is a subject that the daily newspaper usually confines to the legal notices, unless the individual filing is involved with a significant amount of money. For instance, when Anthony De Angelis, the world's largest exporter of fats and oils, put Allied Crude and Vegetable Oil into bankruptcy for $300 million, it was important news, but only because De Angelis could be rated a "success" by virtue of the enormous size of his failure.

Libraries have few books on the subject of consumer bankruptcy, and most of those that they do have are meant only for court officials or lawyers. Most bookstores have none at all.

This book is meant to fill that void.

It defines bankruptcy and explains the various types. It examines the typical bankrupt and analyzes the reasons why he becomes one. And because bankruptcy is only a small part of the whole subject of credit, collection and debt, these topics are surveyed, too.

Most important, the book calls attention to the swelling number of personal bankruptcies. Many experts judge this to be a significant national problem. If it is not, one day soon it will be.

G.S.

THE BOOM
IN GOING BUST

CHAPTER 1

BANKRUPTCY: AN OVERVIEW

Ralph Morse is thirty-three. His wife, Helen, is thirty-one. They have been married twelve years and have a daughter, Linda, who is ten, and a son, Ralph Jr., eight. They live in a three-room, $105-a-month apartment in Long Island City, a grimy section of the borough of Queens in New York City. They are bankrupts.

Ralph sells used cars. Two or three evenings a week he works as a counterman in a bowling alley. When he has a good week—and he does not have too many—he brings home slightly more than $100. The first year the Morses (that is not their real name) were married, Ralph worked for a construction company and earned about $6,500 a year—good wages for a man with no college and virtually no training. The future seemed sparkling bright. The Morses bought a $15,500 house, a year-old sports car, furniture, kitchen appliances—including a home freezer—a stereo system and fishing equipment. "It was a cinch," Helen recalls. "We charged everything we bought but the groceries."

Not long after they had moved into their new home, the Morses owed fourteen creditors a total of $6,900, not including the mortgage. Ralph, still doing construction work, was taking home about $550 a month. Payments were $404, leaving them slightly less than $150 for food and miscellaneous expenses—a fairly precarious situation. But their credit buying continued, and the balance between what was coming in and what was going out grew increasingly delicate. To shore up the family finances, Helen went to work as a sales clerk in a department store. She brought home $50 a week, and things became bright again. But not for long. Ralph traded in the old sports car for a new one. "It cost $3,750," he says, "but I didn't care about that. The salesman worked it out so that the down payment was small and spread out the financing to make it easy on us."

Then came a turning point. Helen got pregnant and had to quit her job. With two pay checks the Morses had barely been able to keep their heads above water. With only one they quickly foundered. When they fell behind on payments, creditors began to hound them. First there were letters, and when they ignored these they were besieged with telephone calls day and night. Sometimes when Ralph came home from work a bill collector's car would be parked in the driveway. When the baby came Ralph went to a finance company and borrowed $700, which went for medical expenses and to still the most persistent of the creditors.

Then the Morses were hit with the unexpected. Ralph was injured on his job and lost several weeks of work. His income halted, he went to a second finance company and managed to get enough money to keep up payments on the car. "I couldn't let them take the car," he said. "It was the only way I had to get to work." Neither bus lines nor subways serviced the area of Long Island where Ralph worked.

When Ralph finally did return to work he learned that his wages had been attached by a loan company. Under New York

State law the garnishment cost him only 10 percent of what he was making, but the paper work involved vexed his employer. "If it happens again," he told Ralph, "you're fired." But Ralph had lost control of the situation by this time. His wages were garnished a second time, and his employer made good his threat.

Ralph got part-time work as a service-station attendant, but his income was scarcely enough to buy food and other necessities. A loan company found out where he was working and his wages were again attached. Then the bank instituted court action to take his house. His car was repossessed. Helen became distraught and the couple quarreled often. Ralph began to stay up nights drinking.

One day Ralph went to see a lawyer and asked him what he should do. As soon as the attorney got an idea of how much Ralph owed, he recommended bankruptcy. Ralph shrugged. He had reached the point where he would do almost anything.

The proceedings were not expensive. They cost him about $350 for everything, including the lawyer's services. Under the lawyer's direction Ralph filed a petition in federal district court. Helen, since she had co-signed a loan agreement and several installment contracts, had to file too. The results were instantaneous. They were not obliged to make any further payments. Bill collectors were restrained from plaguing the couple. Garnishment proceedings were halted. Best of all, it was quick. It took only six weeks for the Morses to be declared bankrupt. They had lost their home, their car—everything but a few pieces of furniture. But they got a fresh start, and that was what they wanted. "It was a tremendous relief," says Ralph.

Bankruptcy is about as old as money and credit, and in the United States it is a constitutional right, one that dates to framing of that document. But never before in the nation's history has the subject been of such concern. Economists, sociologists, lawyers and federal judicial officials are becoming increasingly edgy about the Ralph and Helen Morses of the country.

To some the Morses' conduct was slightly villainous, even fraudulent. They showed themselves to be compulsive buyers. They denied themselves few things they desired. They were unable to distinguish between luxuries and necessities. When they finally became caught up in a great wave of debt, they simply sought sanctuary in bankruptcy court. Says one observer: "Bankruptcy court has increasingly become the dumping ground for the refuse of poorly managed affairs of consumers."

But another view has it that the Morses were simply the victims of all too eager credit extenders. When they became overwhelmed by their credit buying and borrowing, they did no more than what the law allows them to do. In choosing bankruptcy they were merely taking advantage of one of the great humanitarian pieces of legislation of all time.

About people like the Morses, one thing is certain: There are more of them than ever before. Americans are going broke at record rate. According to the Administrative Office of the United States Courts, in the fiscal year 1967 (July 1, 1966, through June 30, 1967) a record total of 208,243 bankruptcy cases were filed in the United States, its territories and the District of Columbia. This was the fifteenth consecutive year in which the number of bankruptcies exceeded the total of the previous year. These year-by-year increases have not been slight. Just a decade ago the total number of bankruptcies was 73,761, about one third of the present annual number.

Here, beginning in fiscal 1948, is a year-by-year summary of bankruptcy filings:

YEAR	NUMBER	NUMERICAL CHANGE	RATE OF CHANGE
1948	18,510	+ 5,340	+ 40.5%
1949	26,021	+ 7,511	+ 40.5%
1950	33,392	+ 7,371	+ 28.3%
1951	35,193	+ 1,801	+ 5.4%
1952	34,873	− 320	− .9%
1953	40,087	+ 5,214	+ 15.0%
1954	53,136	+ 13,049	+ 32.6%
1955	59,404	+ 6,268	+ 11.8%
1956	62,086	+ 2,682	+ 4.5%
1957	73,761	+ 11,675	+ 18.8%
1958	91,668	+ 17,907	+ 24.3%
1959	100,672	+ 9,004	+ 9.8%
1960	110,034	+ 9,362	+ 9.3%
1961	146,643	+ 36,609	+ 33.3%
1962	147,780	+ 1,137	+ .8%
1963	155,493	+ 7,713	+ 5.2%
1964	171,719	+ 16,226	+ 10.4%
1965	180,323	+ 8,604	+ 5.0%
1966	192,354	+ 12,031	+ 6.7%
1967	208,329	+ 15,975	+ 8.3%

Mere growth of population is not the reason that both the number and the rate of bankruptcies are growing so. The incidence of filings has mushroomed as well. In 1950, 22 people out of every 100,000 filed a bankruptcy petition. In 1967, the incidence had risen to 98 out of every 100,000.

These bankruptcies are causing an estimated billion dollars a year to be washed down the drain, a loss reflected in increased interest rates borrowers are charged or consumers pay, or in the cost of merchandise. Often they become the burden of the federal government since they are simply written off on tax returns.

One possible misconception must be cleared away. These figures refer primarily to individuals, not businesses; to employees, not proprietors. In 1967 a startling 92 percent of the total number of bankruptcy filings were of what is often called the consumer type.

These non-business bankruptcies are increasing at a faster rate than bankruptcies as a whole. The total number of filings was about five times higher in 1967 than in 1950. The number of business filings doubled during that period. But the number of consumer bankruptcies was seven times as high.

The government's bankruptcy statistics have their critics, people who claim that the total number of non-business filings is an inflated figure. They say that the difference between what constitutes a business filing and a non-business one can be difficult to perceive, and there are an unrecorded number of filings where one's personal financial distress is brought on by one's business failure. In addition, some of the non-business cases represent instances of a husband and wife filing at the same time and listing virtually the same debts. However, in total, such statistical aberrations are few in number, and they affect the over-all picture hardly at all.

It has become something of a tradition that six states, with about 28 percent of the population, account for more than one half of the country's bankruptcy filings. These states are California, Ohio, Illinois, Alabama, Tennessee and Georgia. They reported about 51 percent of the bankruptcy filings in 1966. They had 55 percent of them five years ago and 59 percent ten years ago.

In many states the skyrocketing rate of bankruptcies is causing considerable anxiety. Consider this evidence:

* In Oregon the number of bankruptcies jumped from 216 in 1946 to 4,860 in 1967. "Bankruptcy has become a habit in Oregon," says Estes Snedecor, a Portland bankruptcy referee. "It seems the proper thing to do."

* In Oklahoma the number of bankruptcies climbed from 700 as recently as 1964 to 3,845 in fiscal 1967, a gain of more

than 500 percent. "Oklahoma is in the grip of a plague, one that exists in the state's court and is known as bankruptcy," said the Tulsa *Tribune*.

* In the Eastern Court District of Missouri, the number of personal bankruptcies has multiplied seven times since 1957. "Credit is easy," says a court official, "and there is tremendous pressure to keep up with affluent neighbors."

* In Kentucky bankruptcy has been characterized as the "in" thing. In the Covington Division of the U.S. District Court there were 4,794 bankruptcy petitions filed in 1967, about three times as many as in fiscal 1957.

* The state of Nevada leads all others in the number of bankruptcies per capita. In 1967 there were 301 filings per 100,000 population. In 1957 there were just 28 per 100,000.

* The Los Angeles *Times* laments the fact that bankruptcy "has become a way of life" in Southern California. Approximately 2,500 people a month file petitions in Los Angeles District Court. Referee Ronald Walker has observed that 90 percent of the bankrupts are wage earners who have simply spent more than they can afford. "They don't know how to handle their money," he says. "They cannot budget. They cannot say no. They are a pushover for the hard-sell guys."

It wasn't many years ago that bankruptcy was regarded as a fairly wicked way to wash out one's indebtedness. Any man who went bankrupt was treated almost as a leper. Women filed about as often as they swam the English Channel. Bankruptcy had a stigma attached to it. It still does, but the scar it leaves isn't nearly so deep as it used to be.

This is not to say that bankruptcy has become the fashion of the day. Not yet. It is still the cause of some chagrin. It is a rare person who actually boasts to his friends about his filing. Robert Dolphin, Jr., who conducted an illuminating analysis of consumer bankrupts in the Flint, Michigan, area, asked respondents to describe how their friends and relatives reacted to the news of their filing. What they said covered a wide range, but a typical response was "Bankruptcy is not a good thing, but in your case it may have been the only way out."

Why the rate of personal bankruptcies is increasing so is a question being asked on several fronts. There are many theories, but no one has a clear-cut answer. Some people say it is the nation's retailers who are at fault by virtue of their improvident credit selling. Others claim it is the fault of the consumer and his uncontrolled itch to spend. A few blame a "new morality," a growing lack of responsibility on the part of some people to pay their debts. The harsh collection laws that some states have on the books are a part of the picture. Some put the blame on the Bankruptcy Act itself. The cause for each individual filing is different, but one of these reasons, or a combination of them, is a factor in almost every single case.

These facts are all important: Never before in the country's history have there been so many and so persistent pressures on people to buy on time and to borrow money. Never before have people used credit so indiscriminatively nor paid such high prices for it.

Between 1946 and 1966 consumer credit, not counting home mortgages, rose from $8.4 billion to $94.8 billion, a spectacular increase. In 1966 interest alone on this debt figure amounted to $12.7 billion. During the same period—1946 through 1966—home mortgages increased from $23 billion to $225 billion.

In the two decades that consumer indebtedness increased tenfold, personal income also went up, but it only tripled. It increased from $147 billion in 1946 to $505 billion in 1966. Whereas in 1946 the consumer had 6 percent of his pay check committed to what he owed, in 1966 one dollar out of every four was so committed.

It is not likely that the pace is going to slacken. The current and long-lived economic boom, which reached its eightieth month in November 1967, was stimulated by the enormous and ever-expanding wave of consumer credit. Surely no one in the federal government is going to line up against credit spending, and neither are the nation's professional moneylenders or retailers. "Sure, we know it's gotten out of hand," says a Chicago banker. "But credit spending is like sin. No one wants to throw the first stone."

America's record spending spree is the backdrop for what is happening on the bankruptcy scene. One other piece of information is significant. Two thirds of the families with installment debt have less than $500 put away for emergencies. Thus, the loss of a job, an accident, an extended illness—any one of these can spell financial disaster.

According to the dictionary, a bankrupt is a "person legally declared unable to pay his debts." A person becomes so declared by filing a bankruptcy petition with a federal court clerk and paying a $50 filing fee. His property, if he has any, is divided among his creditors or administered for their benefit. Most people who file petitions employ attorneys, but one does not have to do so.

Theoretically, any person at all can go bankrupt. The only qualification is that the petitioner must have debts that amount to at least one dollar more than his assets, and he cannot have been granted a discharge within the previous six years.

When he files his petition, the debtor also files schedules which list the names and addresses of his creditors, the amounts owed each and a list of his assets, if he has any assets. The petition is assigned to a bankruptcy court referee who, under the provisions of the National Bankruptcy Act, has much the same power and authority as a federal judge. The court notifies the creditors of the petition and schedules a hearing to give the creditors a chance to oppose the debtor's action.

In the great majority of cases the debtor has no assets, so creditors do not even bother to appear at the hearing. It's a waste of time, they figure, and, since they may have to employ legal counsel, a waste of money too. As a result the debtor is often granted his discharge in routine fashion. This means he is legally free of all his debts except those specified by law, such as taxes or wages earned by someone in his employ.

A debtor's discharge can be thwarted if it can be proven he has acted in a fraudulent manner. A false statement on a loan application or the misrepresentation of facts in making any purchase can constitute a fraud. It is also fraudulent for the petitioner to conceal assets or to attempt to conceal them. If within a year after the discharge has been granted a creditor comes upon new facts concerning possible fraud, he may even then enter an objection. If he is able to prove his case, the discharge can be revoked. However, such action is extremely rare. Again, the reason is that the average creditor feels that the time and effort involved are hardly worth whatever results he might achieve.

A petitioner in bankruptcy court does not lose absolutely everything. Laws in each state detail certain types and amounts of personal property a bankrupt may keep. California is regarded as having the grandest exemption statutes. One has to do with real estate. If the petitioner's equity in his home is under $12,500 and he has filed a "declaration of homestead," the house, even if it is worth $50,000 or more, cannot be seized by creditors. Should the petitioner's equity be more than $12,500, or should he fail to file a homestead declaration, then the house can be taken. But even in the case of a forced sale, the bankrupt gets the first $12,500 to buy another house. The creditors share whatever remains.

The paragraphs above refer to what is called "straight" bankruptcy. About 85 percent of all individuals who file take this course.

People with heavy debt can choose an alternative method of bankruptcy known as "Chapter XIII." Using this course of action, a debtor does not seek release from what he owes. Instead he pays, but he is given an extended period of time to do so.

From a technical standpoint the procedures that one follows in a Chapter XIII case are quite similar to those in a straight voluntary filing. Action is initiated when the debtor files a petition—which is accompanied by a listing of his debts and assets and a statement of his affairs—in federal district court. At the same time he usually files his proposed payment plan, which details precisely how each of his creditors is to be paid. Usually the payments are scheduled over a three-year period. Once the plan is accepted by the creditors and confirmed by the court, the payments begin. All stipulations are carried out under the jurisdiction of the bankruptcy court. Creditors, even the minority who may have opposed the plan, may not exert collection pressure on the debtor as long as he adheres to the repayment schedule.

A small but vocal group of lawyers and referees have become persistent advocates of Chapter XIII proceedings. They feel that it carries out perfectly the intent of bankruptcy legislation. It is of obvious benefit to the creditor. It serves the debtor by helping him to preserve his self-respect, they feel. Thus, Chapter XIII is said to serve the public good.

Linn K. Twinem, chairman of the Bankruptcy Committee of the American Bar Association, is one of the foremost supporters of Chapter XIII. Mr. Twinem declares that he is "shocked" by the ever-increasing number of bankruptcy filings. "The record is even more disturbing," he says, "when it is realized that many of the filings are really not necessary." He cites studies prepared by leading universities which have concluded that from 25 to 50 percent of the people filing bankruptcy could have paid their debts over a period of time if they had been so disposed and so advised. Legislation is now pending before Congress which would require the referee to determine whether a debtor could pay his debts out of future earnings. If the referee decided that he could, the petitioner would be denied straight bankruptcy. He would be able to file only under the provisions of Chapter XIII.

Some referees deride Chapter XIII, and they stamp it as a shrewd weapon of creditor groups to get their money. They also take a dim view of the purported rehabilitative features of the Chapter. "Maybe it does enlighten the debtor on how to handle his income," says one referee, "but this kind of instruction isn't the function of the judiciary. It's something more suited for the Department of Health, Education and Welfare."

The controversy surrounding Chapter XIII is reflected in the erratic pattern of its use. In New York District Court Chapter XIII is employed only on very rare occasions. New York, like many other states, has a proportion of Chapter XIII filings to total bankruptcy cases of less than 1 percent. Yet in other states—Missouri, Iowa, Georgia, Maine, Arkansas and Alabama—the proportion is above 50 percent, and in Alabama it is consistently a whopping 85 percent or thereabouts. In each one of these states there is substantial support for Chapter XIII from court officials, the local bar and creditor community. These groups, cooperating in purposeful way, make Chapter XIII work.

Many of the people who file straight bankruptcy today are similar in circumstances and character to Ralph and Helen Morse. They are about thirty and have young children; they are in a middle-income category. They also are compulsive in their buying habits and have little resistance to the "hard sell." But bankruptcy filings are not limited to just the Ralph and Helen Morses of the country—not by any means. Bankruptcy touches every segment of our society. In a single day recently in New York District Court, petitions were filed by a housewife from Great Neck, a technical writer from Levittown, a music teacher from Mount Vernon and a mechanic from Manhattan.

Well-known people file. Recent petitioners in the world of sports have included a professional golfer, a professional bowler, and football star Carlton (Cookie) Gilchrist of the Denver Broncos. ("It made me feel free," Gilchrist said, "like a man possessed of great, great strength—like my career was just starting.")

Financial difficulties have brought several Hollywood film stars to bankruptcy court in recent years. George Sanders, who said he was "the victim of an international swindle," filed a petition that listed debts of more than a million dollars and negligible assets. Betty Hutton's petition listed debts of $150,000 and practically no assets. "Bankruptcy is the only way out for Betty," said her attorney.

Mickey Rooney's filing was news from coast to coast. People wanted to know how such an eminently successful actor—who had earned more than $12 million in his thirty-year career —could find himself in bankruptcy court. Simple. He listed only $1,500 in assets and a string of debts as long as the Hollywood Freeway. His debtors included a doctor, a car-rental company, two banks, six hotels, seven talent agencies and movie studios, nine lawyers, back alimony and seventeen other creditors. The lowest amount was $200 due a Hollywood hotel; the highest was a loan of $168,000. His indebtedness totaled almost $350,000.

But compared to some others, Mickey Rooney's filing was somewhat petty. Then there is the case of Billie Sol Estes, the Texan who built a vast paper empire by virtue of what investigators called "government favoritism." When Billie Sol filed his bankruptcy petition, his schedules disclosed that he had nearly one thousand creditors, and his debts ranged from 92 cents owed a steel supply company in Plainview to almost

$800,000 due an equipment-finance company in Dallas. Some money due creditors was listed merely as "amount rumored to be involved." It may take a generation of accountants to untangle Billie Sol's financial dealings, and his total indebtedness will probably never be accurately known, but it is believed to be in excess of $50 million. Billie Sol has to be ranked as the "King of the Bankrupts."

At the other end of the scale are people like the Columbus, Ohio, service-station attendant who went bankrupt for a mere $642 in debts, or the Newark, New Jersey, taxi driver who owed less than $800 when he filed. A man in Oregon filed bankruptcy with debts that totaled a mere $199. The filing fee was $50 and he paid a lawyer $150 to handle the case. The cost of his going bankrupt was more than he owed.

It is a fact that bankruptcy is being made increasingly attractive to the nation's poor. In Washington, D.C., leaders of a militant civil-rights organization called ACT—Associated Community Teams—has begun a diligent campaign to inform Negroes of the existence of the bankruptcy law and assist them in filing their petitions. Thousands of ACT leaflets have been distributed in the nation's capital, largely in neighborhoods where small cut-rate "easy credit" jewelry, clothing or furniture stores are to be found. "Eliminate almost all your debts," the leaflets declare, and they point out that the bankruptcy filing fee of $50 is payable in installments "and no down payment is required."

To those who may have a moral timidity about filing, the leaflets say that bankruptcy was "originally derived from the Bible." The following quotation from the Revised Standard Version of the Bible, Deuteronomy 15: 1 and 2, is given: "At the end of every seven years you shall grant a release. And this is the manner of the release: every creditor shall release what he has lent his neighbor; he shall not exact it of his neighbor, his brother, because the Lord's release has been proclaimed."

Retailers and credit managers in Washington are apprehensive. One department-store manager has acknowledged that bankruptcy "could be very effective" for many low-income patrons who have made credit purchases beyond their ability to pay.

"The great untapped benefits of the bankruptcy law to the nation's poor appear to be almost unknown," says an ACT official. "One could reasonably guess that literally tens of thousands of poor persons have a desperate need of the bankruptcy law."

Another effort to reach poor people is being made by a young Fresno, California, couple. They have stirred a statewide controversy by a service they launched to advise people in debt to fight poverty through bankruptcy. Anyce and Tom Hutchinson offer to type bankruptcy papers and schedules for those hopelessly in debt. "But we don't give legal advice," Tom says. "We give sympathy, understanding and guidance." The Hutchinsons have hung posters in stores and laundromats that list their telephone number and proclaim:

> Men and women deep in debt,
> Do not worry, do not fret;
> Uncle Sam has made a way,
> Liquidate instead of pay.

The Hutchinsons themselves went bankrupt in 1960, and their case was quite typical. Twelve years ago they were married and soon had two children. Like most young couples they wanted to enjoy some of the "good things" in life. Credit was the answer. They bought a home, taking out a GI loan. No down payment was needed. They bought a car, furniture and appliances—although Tom's salary was only $80 a week.

"People were only too happy to let us have the stuff," Tom says. "They even kept urging us to buy more."

Then Tom's union went on strike and after that he got sick. Bill collectors besieged the couple. They sought out a financial counselor, who took one look at their assets and liabilities—they owed about $11,000—and advised bankruptcy. Only Tom filed, however, so the creditors then sued Anyce. "It was a mess," Tom says.

"But we did learn one thing about bankruptcy," he states. "It gave us a chance to start all over again. When people come to us for help, we tell them what we did and how we got a second chance."

When the Hutchinsons advertised "Fight Poverty, Go Bankrupt," Fresno's bankruptcy referee, Donald Franson, was flooded with complaints from bankers, finance companies, collection agencies and local attorneys. "We only want to help people in deep financial trouble," Tom says. "I don't favor bankruptcy, but it sure beats a nervous breakdown."

The bankruptcy courts have also become something of a haven for an increasing number of people whose attitude toward credit buying is less than scrupulous. Joseph N. Tilem, Director of Credit for the Hilton Hotels, tells of the young man who obtained a credit card and paid his bills regularly for a year. Then he got into financial difficulty and came to the realization that bankruptcy was the only way out. But before he filed he took a trip to the Caribbean, charging over $4,000 on his credit card. Upon his return he mailed the credit card back to the company and explained that he had to file bankruptcy. He apologized for his conduct.

One day not too long ago a thirty-one-year-old ex-model appeared in bankruptcy court in San Jose, California, to tell how she had managed to accrue 511 different charge accounts over a period of ten years. She had operated with seventeen different aliases. "The Queen of Credit" is what one newspaper called her. Though she had worked intermittently as a $75-a-week medical secretary and had never listed assets of more than $500, she had run up bills at sixty-four clothing and furniture stores with thirty-two doctors, thirty florists, six dentists and several utility companies. It all added up to $86,248 in debt.

No one really knows how often fraud, in whole or in part, motivates bankruptcy proceedings. However, it is generally believed that deliberate or planned bankruptcy is much more prevalent on a business than on a personal level. The racket has won increasing favor among underworld operators. It works like this: A crime syndicate installs a front man in a business operation. Large amounts of merchandise are ordered on credit. The merchandise is sold, but the proceeds are hidden. Then the firm is put into bankruptcy. Often the officers of the corporation will tell the court they simply gambled the money away. Unless this can be disproved and it can be established that the firm is actually concealing its assets, the discharge is granted.

Fraudulent failures are known as "scam" operations. Scam was originally a carnival term meaning to fleece the public. It is estimated that underworld scams in 1965 netted between $50 and $75 million and that this amount was equalled by free-lance amateurs engaged in the same swindle.

In the largest of the most recent business bankruptcy fraud cases involving professionals, a federal district court in New York City convicted six persons of conspiring to transfer $1.3 million in assets at the expense of creditors. The meat and poultry business was the setting for the swindle. One defendant, identified by the Justice Department as a member of the Cosa Nostra, took over control of a financially disabled meat and poultry packing company. He operated the firm by ordering substantial quantities of meat and poultry and selling much of it to a wholesale meat and poultry company whose owner was also, according to authorities, a Cosa Nostra member. The Justice Department charged that during one ten-day period the wholesaler paid the packing company more than $75,000, but no money could be found when creditors started involuntary bankruptcy proceedings against the defendant.

The Justice Department has embarked on a campaign against planned bankruptcies, but relatively few are reported and brought to prosecution. One reason is that the marked increase in the total number of bankruptcies—both business and personal—forces many courts to rush cases without examining them for possibilities of fraud. During 1964 and 1965, federal agencies investigated 1,600 suspicious bankruptcies, but only 89 convictions resulted.

● The word *bankruptcy* dates to early-day Italy and to a time when bankers and money-changers conducted their affairs from benches or stalls on the Italian bourse. When one failed or became insolvent, his bench was destroyed, and the name *banco-rotto*, or "broken-bench," was given to him. To the French, the word became *banqueroute;* to the English, banker-out. In time it became "bankrupt."

The very nature of trade and commerce, which are founded on credit and great debt, demand a bankruptcy system. When a debtor fails, his property, in moral justice, belongs to his creditors. Bankruptcy law dictates this and, further, that it is to be divided ratably among them. Every commercial country in the world has some form of bankruptcy.

● The earliest English statute on the subject of bankruptcy dates to 1542. It granted not the slightest relief to the debtor but merely authorized seizure by the Crown of the debtor's assets and provided that they could be divided among those whom he owed.

In accordance with the authority granted by the Constitution, Congress has enacted five major statutes concerning bankruptcy. The first was passed by the Federalists in 1800 but was repealed just three years later by the Jefferson Administration because it was said to overly favor the mercantile class. The country was without bankruptcy legislation until 1841. The bill passed that year was very broad in scope and stressed not only creditor protection but debtor relief as well, a provision that quickly came to be regarded as immoral. In 1843 the measure was repealed. A statute passed in 1867 expanded the provisions that authorized discharge from debt, but it was struck down in 1879 due to creditor opposition. The panic of 1893 gave rise to the bankruptcy statute enacted in 1898. It has undergone extreme change but it has never been repealed. Significant revisions came with the passage of the Chandler Act in 1938, which provided important rehabilitative provisions for individuals.

The attitude of rehabilitation is prevalent, too, in bankruptcy legislation dealing with businesses. While business bankruptcies are not the concern of this book, two types are worth mentioning. Chapter X of the Bankruptcy Act is meant for businessmen in financial difficulty who wish to refinance and reorganize their corporation without interrupting operations. It is often used in the case of publicly owned corporations. The judge appoints a trustee if the liabilities exceed $250,000, and the trustee is responsible to the stockholders and debenture holders. In Chapter XI proceedings the corporation works out "arrangements" with creditors under the supervision of the court. Extensions of time are granted for the payment of unsecured debts or the debts are reduced in size, or both. Unincorporated may also avail themselves of the relief offered by Chapter XI.

More than rehabilitative features, what is unique about the

American system of bankruptcy is that it grants the honest debtor a release from his obligations, an unconditional release. The legal systems of Italy, France, Belgium and Argentina provide that a non-business debtor can be granted a discharge, but only if he enters into a composition arrangement with his creditors—that is, only if he agrees to pay them a part of what he owes. In Denmark, Sweden, Austria and Germany a consumer may file a bankruptcy petition and obtain a release from his debt, but it is conditioned on his paying them a reduced amount over an extended period. In England and most Commonwealth countries the debtor's discharge is also similarly conditioned.

The United States is wholly atypical in its attitude toward the debtor. But this is not to suggest that our system is at all improper. The pressure of debt is fierce and persistent. Bankruptcy, while often described as a "last resort," is not; it is only one of a number of courses an insolvent may choose. Some appeal to their families for help. Some skip, abandoning their families and jobs along with their problems. A few steal. A good number adjust and remain in involuntary servitude to their creditors for all of their lives. Bankruptcy is the humane way out.

CHAPTER 2

HOW IT STARTED

There is complete agreement among scholars that our statutes concerning bankruptcy come from "the one great fundamental principle that when a person's property is insufficient to pay in full all of his creditors, it shall be divided equally pro rata among them." So states William Miller Collier in his formidable text *The Law and Practice of Bankruptcy*. This concept is rooted in the most ancient of legal sytems.

In primitive society there were no laws that might be interpreted as relating to insolvency or bankruptcy as we know these concepts today, for the simple reason that debtors and creditors were unknown in the early stages of social evolution. Primitive man had little or no faith in his neighbor. When one man delivered goods to another, payment was immediate and in full. As social systems matured, the theory of credit was gradually introduced. At first it was merely a suspension of payment privilege; but it was held in the highest regard, and even the slightest violation occasioned the harshest penalties, whether the defaulting debtor was adjudged to be acting fraudulently or not.

It was usual that a hopeless debt was satisfied by labor or physical punishment or both.

23

In Hindu law, for example, the creditor could seize the debtor and compel him to work for him. He could—lawfully—maim or kill the debtor, "or confine his wife, sons or cattle or besiege him in his home."

Another device practiced in ancient India and still favored in parts of Nepal was known as "sitting d'harna," wherein the creditor sat and fasted on the debtor's doorstep until the debt was paid. A similar practice, known as "fasting on," was resorted to in ancient Ireland. Such collection methods were strikingly successful. As the starving creditor approached exhaustion, a rising wave of public protest demanded that the debtor discharge his obligation.

There are a number of biblical references testifying to the fact that one could be enslaved for the non-payment of debt. This account is from the Old Testament (IV Kings 4:1): ". . . a certain woman of the wives of the prophets came to Elisha saying: 'Thy servant, my husband is dead and thou knowest that thy servant was one that feared God, and behold the creditor has come to take away my two sons to serve him.' " Elisha told the woman, "Go outside, borrow vessels of all your neighbors . . ." Then from a single vessel of oil she filled all the vessels that had been gathered. Then Elisha said to her, "Go sell the oil and pay thy debt . . ."

In the Gospel of St. Matthew (18:23–25), the kingdom of heaven is compared to a king who wished to settle accounts with his servants. "When he began the reckoning," states the narrative, "one was brought to him who owed him ten thousand talents; and as he could not pay, his lord ordered him to be sold, with his wife and children and all that he had, and payment to be made."

In ancient Greece the criminal code of Draco (623 B.C.) classified indebtedness with murder, sacrilege and other capital crimes. Later this stricture was tempered, and debtors were

merely compelled to remain on the creditor's land and to culti-
vate it and to surrender their children to be exported as slaves.
Solon, during his reign, revised the Draconian codes and put
an end to the practice of enslaving freemen. He ordered that
what debts remained after an attempt at restitution should be
forgiven but that the insolvent and his heirs had to forfeit their
citizenship. To the people of ancient Greece this was a deep
loss; one's citizenship was almost as precious as life itself.

The law of ancient Rome, as set forth in the *Laws of the
Twelve Tables* and promulgated in 451 or 450 B.C., declared
that the borrower was *nexus* to his creditor, which meant that
his own person was pledged for repayment of the loan. If
the borrower failed to fulfill his obligation, the creditor could
seize him. Then, after publicly inviting someone to come forth
to pay the debt and no one did, the creditor could regard the
debtor as his slave. He could kill him or sell him. He usually
did the latter. The proverb "He who cannot pay with his purse,
pays with his skin" had a ruthlessly literal application in early
times.

Gradually this notion changed. In time restitution, not
vengeance, grew to be paramount. Execution was directed not
against the debtor himself but against his property, and the
evolving systems of Jewish, Germanic and Roman law clearly
demonstrate this.

In much of the insolvency legislation through the centuries,
one problem has prevailed: In the case where a debtor's estate
has several creditors, which one is to be paid first? In most
early systems creditors were ranked in order of time, with the
oldest claim being settled first. In some systems, however, the
ranking of creditors was determined by the nature of their
claims.

When all the creditors were of the same rank, it was common
to divide the property *pro rata* among them. But Jewish law

was an exception. In instances where the creditors were of equal rank, the estate of the debtor was divided *equally* among them. For example, if a debtor's estate amounted to $1,500 and there were three claimants to it, all of equal rank and each with minimum claims of $500, each would receive $500. This system made it possible to pay a high percentage of smaller debts and was based upon the Talmud, wherein the rabbis declared that if a man dies leaving three widows, each one is to share equally in his estate.

The liberalization of ancient laws of insolvency are also marked by a growing ability to draw a distinction between the debtor who was dishonest and the one who was honest but unfortunate. Under Islamic law a certain portion of the honest debtors were declared exempt from seizure by his creditors. The Code of Hammurabi, a ruler of Babylonia beginning in 1750 B.C., stands as landmark legislation in the moderating of insolvency laws. "The strong shall not injure the weak" was the guiding principle of Hammurabi's reign. "Let the farmer who owes the corn, but cannot pay, produce all his goods before witnesses and give them to the merchant," the code dictated. "The merchant shall take them as full payment of the debt. But if the witnesses value the debtor's goods to be more than what is owed, then the merchant shall take only enough goods to satisfy the debt. If the merchant takes more than is due him or illegally seizes the property of the farmer, then the merchant shall be punished according to law. If the debtor conceals his property, or fails to produce all of it, then he shall be punished."

This compassion toward the debtor was also typical of later Roman Law. In Rome of 326 B.C., the *Lex Poetalia* stated that a debtor, by swearing that his assets equalled his liabilities, and surrendering his property, could maintain his freedom and escape the hardship of the *Laws of the Twelve Tables*.

Rome's Corpus Juris Civilis, promulgated by the Christian emperor Justinian in 533, provided the first really charitable treatment of the debtor. It stated that if a debtor yielded up all his property to his creditors, he was not to be imprisoned. But debtors of the day abused their privilege. To be released from the necessity of paying, they falsely swore they were unable to pay. But the law did not remain in existence for long. Rome was crumbling. The legal system, like almost everything else, fell into disuse and decay. But what is important is that the influence of Roman law, in its just but liberal attitude toward the debtor, carried to England.

Laws concerning insolvency in England date to the thirteenth century, a time that marked the dawning of the nation's commercial life. No less a document than the Magna Carta, granted by King John in 1215, declared it was illicit to seize the land and property of a debtor when his personal goods were sufficient to pay his debts, and he was willing to surrender them to his creditors. For years after the English legal system would not allow a person to be imprisoned or otherwise set upon for debt. Only a debtor's property could be taken to satisfy a claim. Such liberality was not only a carry-over from the Roman system of Corpus Juris Civilis of a time seven centuries before, but such charity may also have been proof of the deep influence wielded by ecclesiastical authorities of the day.

From the Jews, who came to England as serfs to the king following the Norman conquest in 1066, and from the Lombards, too, the English learned to borrow and lend money and to extend and receive credit for goods. Bills of exchange, letters of credit and currency came into widespread use. Commercial growth and trade—exports primarily—were the nation's policy by the fifteenth century.

Against this background Henry VIII in 1542 brought into

being legislation that bore a close resemblance to certain portions of our own latter-day bankruptcy code. His motive was to encourage his country's commercial growth by discouraging misrepresentation and fraud. The statute applied to the merchant class exclusively and it empowered the Lord Chancellor and other high officials to seize the assets of an insolvent and distribute them for the benefit of his creditors. It was, then, a form of involuntary bankruptcy. Debtors themselves could not decide to go bankrupt; it had to be thrust upon them by their creditors. And there was not the slightest hint of discharge in the law. Its sole aim was to protect the creditor from the dishonest debtor.

Under Queen Elizabeth the application of the law was broadened so as to include "bankers, brokers and scriveners," and in 1706, during the reign of George II, the law was further liberalized, allowing bankrupts to keep certain valuables. F. Regis Noel, in *A History of the Bankruptcy Clause of the Constitution,* says that this may have been the origin of the principle of exemption. Exempt assets are those which, under state law, are not subject to the claim of bankruptcy court.

In colonial America, bankruptcy law took somewhat the same tack as English law. The colonies, however, did not pass any statutes that were known technically as "bankruptcy" laws. Instead, they had insolvent laws. Any person who was imprisoned for debt could be granted a release on the surrender of all his property to his creditors. But if further debt still existed, he was not released from it.

Colonial legislation did not distinguish between insolvency and bankruptcy. As Mr. Justice Story, writing in 1833, stated: "Bankrupt law may contain those regulations which are generally found in insolvent laws; and insolvent laws may contain those which are common to bankrupt laws."

In the earliest days of the colonies there was little need for insolvency legislation. Few debts were ever contracted, and any that might have been were paid promptly. In Massachusetts—indeed, through all of New England—a rigid code of public conduct was in force. A prodigal debtor was socially ostracized or, worse, banished.

When laws were instituted they showed little mercy toward the debtor. The only way one could obtain a release from one's indebtedness was to pay. For example, in Virginia the law stated "a debtor can liberate his body from imprisonment by assigning over his estate, both real and personal, for the benefit of the creditor." The debtor could not be imprisoned again for the same debt, but if the property given over to the creditor was not sufficient to pay the debt, any subsequent property the debtor might acquire was subject to attachment by the creditor.

In other states the law was similar. North Carolina passed a constitutional provision that stated that "the person of the debtor, where there is not a strong presumption of fraud, shall not be continued in prison after delivering up, bona fide, all his estate, real and personal, for the use of his creditors. . . ." Here was the principle of insolvency, pure and clear.

In the years that followed the American Revolution, the crime of debt was exceedingly common. According to John Bach McMaster in his monumental study *The History of the People of the United States from the Revolution to the Civil War*, more people were imprisoned for debt than for any other reason. "The class most likely to get into debt," says McMaster, "was the most defenseless and dependent, the great body of servants and artisans, and of laborers, those in short who depended on their daily wages for their daily bread. The laborer who fell from a scaffold or lay sick of the fever was sure to be seized the moment he recovered, and be carried to the jail for the bill of a few dollars which had run up during his illness at the huckster's or the tavern."

The law of the day was harsh on the debtor, but prison was

sheer horror. Newgate Prison, near Granby, Connecticut, had been an abandoned copper mine and was accessible only by a ladder that had been strung down the main shaft. At one time it held as many as one hundred debtors. Their feet were fastened to iron bars, and they were chained by their necks to beams in the roof. Says McMaster: "The darkness was intense; the cave reeked with filth; vermin abounded; water trickled from the roof and oozed from the sides of the caverns; huge masses of earth were continually falling off. In the dampness and the filth the clothing of the prisoners grew mouldy and rotted away, and their limbs became stiff with rheumatism."

Newgate Prison was probably the worst of all, but others were almost as bad. A prison in Northampton, Massachusetts, had cells less than four feet in height. Worcester, in the same state, had a prison with "keeps" that had no means of ventilation. In a prison dungeon in Philadelphia, inmates were penned in like cattle, without beds or bedding, and given scarcely enough food to sustain life.

Prisons were not the only means of punishment of the day. Edward Channing, in his *History of the United States*, declares that ". . . the pillory and whipping post worked overtime, ears were cropped and amputated; the tread-mill turned continuously; the lash fell harshly and unmercifully on the backs of the innocent; the shears dripped with blood and the branding iron emitted the stench of burning human flesh."

John Fiske, in *The Critical Period of American History*, has also described the pitiable condition of the debtor during these times. Says Fiske: "High minded but unfortunate men were carried to jail, and herded with thieves and ruffians in loathsome dungeons for the crime of owing a hundred dollars which they could not promptly pay." Such treatment, he says, ". . . tended to make the debtor an outlaw, ready to entertain schemes for the subversion of society."

These were conditions that existed in the United States under the Articles of Confederation. Later, Daniel Webster would characterize the period in these words: "A vicious system of legislation, a system of paper money and tender laws, had completely paralyzed industry, threatened to beggar every man of property and ultimately ruin the country. The relation between debtor and creditor, always delicate and always dangerous when it divides society . . . was in such condition . . . as to threaten an overthrow of all government, and a revolution was menaced, much more critical and alarming than that through which the country had recently passed."

The Articles served a valuable purpose in providing for a "perpetual union" and a "firm league of friendship" between the states, but they were wretchedly inadequate in regulating commerce among the colonies. The financial and industrial condition of America sank to a low ebb. By the end of 1786, the Articles were in general discredit, and national leaders were seeking a whole new basis of union.

CHAPTER **3**

"CONGRESS SHALL HAVE THE POWER"

The federal government regulates bankruptcy in the United States. It has always had the power to do so. Article I, Section 8, Clause 4 of the Constitution provides that "the Congress shall have the power . . . to establish uniform laws on the subject of bankruptcies throughout the United States."

The framers of the Constitution realized that to a commercial country bankruptcy statutes are as necessary as stable currency. James Madison wrote in *The Federalist* (No. 42): "The power of establishing uniform laws of bankruptcy is so intimately connected with the regulation of commerce and will prevent so many frauds where the parties or their property may be or be removed into different States that the expediency of it seems not likely to be drawn into question."

On August 29, 1787, a date very late in proceedings of the Constitutional Convention, Charles Pinckney of South Carolina moved to commit Article XVI (the Full Faith and Credit clause) but with the provision that power also be granted "To establish uniform laws on the subject of bankruptcies, and respecting the damages arising in the protest of foreign bills of exchange."

32

Two days later John Randolph came forth with the recommendation that the subject of bankruptcies be included in Article VII, which related to the legislature. Randolph advised that after the power "To establish a uniform rule of naturalization throughout the United States" should be added a power "To establish uniform rules on bankruptcies." On September 4, with almost no debate, the Randolph suggestion was adopted. The vote was ten to one, Connecticut voting the lone "Nay." Historians claim that Connecticut's opposition was due to the fact that the state had its own bankruptcy law and there was feeling that the federal regulation might cause conflict.

The bankruptcy clause was not discussed on the floor of the convention again. (In the Report of the Committee on Style and, as a result, in the final draft of the Constitution, the bankruptcy clause was made a part of Article I, Section 8, which enumerates the powers of Congress.) It was adopted as part of the Constitution on September 17, 1787.

Despite the clear-cut mandate granted by the Constitution, the nation has spent more years without a bankruptcy act than with one. Before 1898, the year that marked the passage of the act that is law today, bankruptcy legislation was operative for a total of only sixteen years.

In the first years of the United States, the federal government had problems to consider much more pressing than that of bankruptcy. On June 1, 1789, just two months after the beginning of the first session of the House of Representatives, a committee of the House was named to prepare a bankruptcy bill, but the move was tabled. William Smith, a representative from South Carolina, reported that preparing a law on the subject was an "intricate and perplexing business." He proposed that action on the bill be deferred "until the public debt was funded and banks established, without which it was difficult to conceive how arrangements could be made to facilitate the payment of debts or the operation of such law."

Representative Smith felt the insolvent acts of the various states would suffice in the meantime.

Before long, however, the passage of a bankruptcy bill became an urgent matter. The economic prosperity that characterized the early years of the federal government developed into a great wave of speculation by 1791. Schemes for internal improvements—canals, turnpikes, and manufacturing and mining projects—were rife, and wild speculation in government scrip and bank stocks reached pandemic proportions. A disastrous collapse followed. When it came Thomas Jefferson estimated the "dead loss" in New York to be five million dollars, "which is reckoned," he said, "the value of all buildings of that city, so that the whole town had been burnt to the ground it would have been the measure of the present calamity."

The country's commercial life sagged to a halt. New construction stopped. The number of unemployed spiraled upward, while prices for farm goods slid down.

Thus a bankruptcy bill was reported in the Second Congress, which convened in 1790, with the idea that such a bill would help to relieve the dire financial and economic conditions of the day. However, no action was taken on the measure, and in ensuing years other bills similarly failed.

The year 1797 saw increased financial chaos. Again speculation, primarily in real estate, was the cause. This was the period that saw the rise of such infamous groups as the North American Land Company, which owned six million acres in New York, Pennsylvania and sections of the South; the Miami Purchase in Ohio of John Cleves Symmes; John Duer's Scioto Associates, which also operated in Ohio; and the District of Columbia Syndicate. The most notorious of all was the Yazoo Fraud, a scheme wherein the Georgia legislature granted thirty million acres, covering most of the present states of Alabama and Mississippi, to groups of people, some of whom were members of the selfsame legislative body that did the granting. Almost all of these enterprises failed, and the principals were liable to the stockholders.

A majority of the states did not have insolvency laws, and so these speculators were imprisoned for their debts. William Duer died in debtor's prison in New York. Robert Morris, a principal financier of the American Revolution, languished in Prune Street jail in Philadelphia, and James Wilson, later a justice of the U.S. Supreme Court, had to flee to North Carolina to prevent his imprisonment in Pennsylvania.

The need for a national bankruptcy law was more pressing than ever before. But when a bill was introduced in the first session of the Fifth Congress there was uncompromising resistance to it. Federalist legislators representing the industrial North wanted it; those from the agricultural South were the ones who opposed it. This alignment continued for generations.

Representatives from Virginia, among those who objected to the bill, voiced a view that was fairly typical. They felt that a federal bankruptcy law would make it possible for a creditor to lay claim to their land should they, through no fault of their own, be forced to default on an obligation. The advocates of the bill, all representing commercial interests, included Robert G. Harper of South Carolina, who introduced the legislation in the House; Charles Pinckney of South Carolina; Harrison Gray Otis and Samuel Sewall of Massachusetts; and James Bayard of Delaware. The bill lost by a close vote and was promptly reintroduced in the next Congress in 1799.

By this time the need for a bankruptcy law had grown even more imperative. Besides the financial turmoil caused by the land speculations, there had been additional damage wrought to the country's financial structure through a brief rupture in Franco-American relations that saw the French seizing and plundering American merchant vessels. During this period Jefferson wrote to James Madison, "The whole commercial race are lying on their oars and gathering in their affairs, not knowing what failure may put their resources to the proof."

Against this backdrop the country's first bankruptcy legislation came into being. It was passed in the House on February 21, 1800, by a single vote, 49 to 48, that cast by the Speaker, Thomas Sedgwick of Massachusetts. The vote was 16 to 12 in the Senate.

The Bankruptcy Act of 1800 was extremely mild by today's standards. It was a purely involuntary measure—that is, a case could be initiated only by one's creditors and a discharge granted only when two thirds of one's creditors gave consent.

When the act was voted into law, Congress specified that it was to be limited to five years' existence; but it lasted less time than that. It was abolished in November 1803, with a heavy majority in both the House and the Senate favoring repeal.

No great public outcry accompanied the cancellation of the act, for it never achieved wide favor. Scarcely 500 people in New York, Pennsylvania, Maryland and the District of Columbia were thrust into bankruptcy during the tenure of the law, and these were the states where bankruptcy was most common. In general, the bill was repealed because it was thought to benefit rich debtors and speculators, as well as fraudulent debtors, who were able to exercise the discharge provision by having a friendly creditor initiate action against them. Once being freed from debt, they resumed their financial machinations.

Creditors had no great regard for the act either. Most of the debtors had no assets, a fact that the crowded prisons attested to, and so the distribution feature of law availed them next to nothing. The act was also in general disfavor because of the inconvenience it imposed by necessitating travel to federal court. There was resentment, too, among those legislators who felt that bankruptcy was not a federal matter, that state insolvent laws, where they existed, could serve. Many people much preferred the state system because state laws applied to any insolvent, not just traders.

For a time commercial prosperity alleviated any critical need for a national bankruptcy code, but the good times were brief. In 1806 the French Decrees and the English Orders of Council, by virtue of which these foreign powers confiscated American shipping, brought heavy losses to the merchants of New York and New England. The Embargo and the Non-Intercourse Acts under Presidents Jefferson and Madison caused further commercial strangulation.

Soon the jails were overflowing with debtors. In 1809 and again in 1812, new appeals were launched in Congress for a bankruptcy law, but to no avail. Then the situation worsened. In April 1814 a decision was handed down in U.S. Circuit Court that held an insolvency law in Pennsylvania to be unconstitutional—first, because it discharged debts incurred by contracts dated prior to the law itself, and, second, on the grounds that only Congress had the power to pass legislation discharging debts. Then in 1819 the U.S. Supreme Court, in *Sturgis vs. Crownshield,* held that the New York State insolvent law of 1811 was unconstitutional as it applied to prior contracts. Consternation swept the financial world. Now seemingly there was no way in which a debtor could obtain a release from his obligations and the resultant siege in prison. "The decision renders the passage of a national law imperious," declared the Baltimore *American.* "The apathy that prevails in Congress on the subject is really surprising. How long will they shut their ears against the cries of distress? How long will they neglect the supplications of thousands?"

The War of 1812 further jarred the American economy, and

it was followed by a depression of almost paralyzing proportions. Many banks suspended specie payments; prices fell,
and debtors increased their clamor for relief. Speaking in
the Senate, James Buchanan described the years of 1819,
1820 and 1821 as "the most disastrous which the country ever
experienced since the adoption of the Federal Constitution."

In 1820 bankruptcy legislation was introduced in the Senate
to provide debtors with the relief they so sorely needed. As
the measure was being debated, a significant turning point
occurred. Senator Nicholas Van Dyke of Delaware proposed
an amendment providing that *any person* imprisoned for debt
might voluntarily file a petition to be adjudged a bankrupt.
"Now," says Charles Warren in *Bankruptcy in United States
History,* "for the first time in the history of the world legislation was proposed to benefit debtors at large instead of merely
to enable creditors to reach the property of merchants and
traders."

Van Dyck's proposal, receiving strong support from Henry
Clay, passed in the Senate, 25–16, but the bill itself was voted
down. Oddly, it was the Northern Senators who caused its
defeat, for they believed that the Van Dyck amendment was
unconstitutional, that bankruptcy legislation could apply only
to merchants and traders.

In the next Congress, in 1822, the struggle continued. A
proposal similar to Van Dyck's was introduced in the House,
stating that voluntary bankruptcy might apply to all debtors
so long as their creditors assented. This brought forth all the
old arguments—that it would "lay an axe" to the root of the
freehold system, that it was an undue extension of the jurisdiction of the federal government, and that, succinctly, it was
unconstitutional. This bill was defeated too.

In 1826 those who favored a bankruptcy law proposed a
piece of legislation that contained a simple and clever com-

promise. It provided for a form of voluntary bankruptcy under which a creditor might petition into bankruptcy any person other than a trader, but only with the assent of the debtor. No longer would those who opposed the legislation be able to claim that it favored the mercantile class and was discriminatory to farmers.

However, the bill was heatedly attacked on other grounds. It was said to be an insolvency law, not a bankruptcy statute, and therefore in the domain of the states, not the federal government. Senator Levi Woodbury of New Hampshire called it a "dangerous" measure. He asked: "What farmer in the Federal Convention of 1787 ever dreamed that he was confessing such a power in Congress over anybody but merchants?" Early in 1827 the bill was voted down. So decisively was it defeated, and so strong was the feeling that voluntary bankruptcy was not constitutional, that no further action on bankruptcy legislation was taken for more than a decade.

Not many weeks after the bankruptcy bill was beaten in Congress, the Supreme Court handed down a 4–3 decision which upheld the power of the various states to enact insolvency laws applying to future contracts—a reversal of the court's previous position. This action strengthened the cause of those who opposed national bankruptcy legislation and became an additional reason for Congress' lack of action.

One other reason was that the status of the debtor was improving. One by one the states were repealing legislation that made prison mandatory for debt. Kentucky was the first to do this—in 1821. Other states followed in ensuing years, and by 1857, when Massachusetts put an end to imprisonment for debt, almost all the other states had so acted. This trend made the necessity for a national bankruptcy law much less pressing.

The subject of bankruptcy was not again seriously consid-

ered in the Congress until 1837, a year in which the country
was beset by the "Great Panic." The early 1830s were years of
unhealthy expansion. The states piled up huge debts in the
construction of canals and railroads and in the chartering of
new banks. Land speculation, given impetus by generous
credit policies, was widespread. The end came abruptly. On
July 11, 1836, President Jackson, in an effort to halt the great
wave of speculation, issued his Specie Circular which required
all payments for public land to be made in gold and silver.
Previously, and with the same motive, Congress had passed
the Deposit Act, and this provided for a distribution of Treas-
ury surplus funds to depository banks, causing them to contract credit. Coinciding with these two pieces of legislation, a
financial crisis struck England, and British creditors began to
call in their loans. That was not all. At the same time American
farmers were hit by severe crop failures. The result of all of
this was an acute depression that lasted seven years. "It just
seems impossible that conditions can ever right themselves
enough to have prosperous times in this country again," said
Daniel Webster. "Trade and industry throughout the land
are disorganized. Banks by the hundreds have failed. Securities
have fallen to one half or even one quarter of their former
values. The problem of unemployment has become general,
and in all large cities special committees have been organized
to provide food and clothing for the poor and unemployed. In
addition to this effort, some cities have caused relief work to
be instigated by public bodies. Widespread want and distress
have led to labor strikes."

The dreadful economic situation spurred President Van
Buren to urge the passage of a bankruptcy bill in his Special
Message delivered to Congress late in 1837. But Van Buren
wanted such legislation confined to banks, and for that reason
it met bitter opposition from Congress.

As the depression worsened, the urgency for a debtor relief

measure grew more critical. In 1840 Daniel Webster introduced in Congress a bill which provided for involuntary bankruptcy in the case of traders and voluntary bankruptcy for "all persons whatsoever owing debts." However, when the bill was reported out of the Judiciary Committee, the involuntary provision had been struck out. The voluntary provision was all that remained.

A great hue and cry was raised as a consequence. Garrett Wall of New Jersey called the proposed law "a general jubilee for debtors," and Henry Hubbard of New Hampshire declared that the bill was "admirably calculated in favor of dishonest debtors and rogues." Thomas Hart Benton was another and heated opponent of the measure. He denounced it in terms that have somewhat of a modern ring: "It will teach the rising generation a facile way to get rid of their obligations after squandering the money and property which they had obtained on the faith of paying for it."

But no phrase-maker of the day could match the eloquence of Daniel Webster, the bill's staunchest supporter. "I verily believe," he declared, "that the power of perpetuating debts against debtors, for no substantial good to the creditor himself, and the power of imprisonment for debt, at least as existed in this country ten years ago, have imposed more restraint on personal liberty than the law of debtor and creditor imposes on any other Christian country." Webster's persuasive oratory carried the day. The bill, again revised to include an involuntary provision as well as a voluntary one, was passed in the Senate, though it was too late in the session for the House to act.

But the next year—1841—the advocates of a national bankruptcy law achieved victory. An important factor was the support that the voluntary feature of the bill received from the Whig party.

The Whigs, with William Henry Harrison as their candidate,

were victorious in the presidential elections of 1840. The campaign they staged that year was unique for the great popular and emotional support it generated in its appeal to "the common man." The passage of a bankruptcy law was one of the issues in this campaign.

It was estimated that there were 400,000 insolvents in the country at the time, and thus Whig support of a voluntary bankruptcy law played an influential role in that party's success. Charles Warren points out that the bankruptcy issue may have been what turned the tide for the Whigs in five states with 89 electoral votes and which the Whigs carried by only 18,000 popular votes.

With the Whigs in power, Senator John McPherson Berrien of Georgia introduced the same bankruptcy statute which had passed in the previous session. It was passed on July 25, 1841. The vote was 26 to 23.

But great opposition loomed in the House. Northern Whigs took exception to the clause that made the bill applicable to banking corporations, and there was also resistance to the voluntary bankruptcy feature. Said Representative Joseph Trumbull of Connecticut: "Voluntary bankruptcy is a new term. Who ever heard such language before? Under this bill the discharge of the debtor is the thing principally aimed at. Under previous acts, surrender of property was the chief object."

Many of those who favored a national law did so because of the assorted inequities in state insolvency statutes. For instance, when a debtor failed it was usual for an out-of-state creditor to get nothing at all.

But the opposition was great, and on August 17, 1841, a motion to table the bill was carried in the House by a vote of 110 to 97. The act appeared doomed, at least for that session. Then came a startling turn of events. The very next day a motion to reconsider the measure was introduced and carried. Then the bill itself was reintroduced and promptly voted into law, 110–106. In the hours between the tabling of the bill and its ultimate passage some astute political bargaining had taken place. Opponents of the bill from Western states were induced to switch their votes in return for votes that would assure passage of the Distribution Bill, one that provided for the dealing out of certain government lands. Seldom before had the art of logrolling been carried to such heights.

Thus, after a lapse of thirty-eight years, the country had a bankruptcy law, its second, and the very first to provide for the voluntary form of bankruptcy. The law went into effect on February 1, 1842.

Despite the fact that it worked with some degree of success, the Bankruptcy Act of 1841 quickly became unpopular. Creditors disliked it because they saw debtors repudiating money they owed and with no thought of repayment. Debtors objected to the act because it did not preserve any of the property exemptions that state statutes allowed, though the bill did support state liens.

Thomas Hart Benton, inveterate foe of the measure, introduced legislation for repeal in 1843. Benton had urged repeal even before the bill had become operative, but his motion had been rejected. Now the climate was much more in his favor. He charged that the legislation was unconstitutional, that "Congress has no inherent or supreme authority over debts. It cannot abolish debts as it pleases," he said. "The attempts to do so are despotism, such as can only be looked for in a government which has no limit in its moral or political powers."

The bill to repeal was passed in both the House and the Senate by substantial margins, in the House by 171–140 and in the Senate by 32–13. Thus the second bankruptcy act passed from the scene. It had not lasted much more than one year. But unlike the previous piece of legislation, the Bankruptcy Act of 1841 was put to ample use. A total of 33,379 persons took advantage of its provisions. The amount of debt involved was $440,934,000, while debtors surrendered property valued at $43,697,357.

Though the bill was short-lived, its effects are felt to this day. It established as law the principle of voluntary bankruptcy, and this principle was affirmed by the Supreme Court. Though the court never did consider in specific terms whether this provision was in accordance with the Constitution, it decided several cases that had to do with the statutory construction of the act, and by so doing acknowledged its constitutionality as a whole. As Charles Warren points out, after the Civil War, when bankruptcy legislation was next considered in Congress, the provision of voluntary bankruptcy was completely and wholly regarded as being within the constitutional power of Congress. It was accepted to such a degree that it was not even the subject of debate.

The years that followed the repeal of the Bankruptcy Act of 1841 were years of wide prosperity, and there was no urgency for bankruptcy legislation. Besides, debtors were gaining more and more protection from the laws of the various states. Some now forbade foreclosure on a debtor's land unless the land could be sold for as much as two-thirds of its appraised value. And additional states were passing insolvency legislation. Some of these worked to the advantage of the debtor and some heavily favored the creditor, but, all in all, the public found them satisfactory.

When there was agitation for national bankruptcy legislation again it was caused, as it always had been before, by hard times—specifically, the Panic of 1857. The country had enjoyed more than a decade of booming prosperity, and again it was a period characterized by wholesale speculation, this time largely in railroad construction. The discovery of gold in California and the ensuing rush to the gold fields contributed to the reckless spirit of the times. The bubble burst with the failure of the Ohio Life Insurance Company of Cincinnati in 1857. The depression spread from the Ohio Valley into the industrial areas of the Northeast and the wheat belt of the West and then into the South, though the cotton states, because farm prices remained stable, were less affected than most.

As unemployment grew and breadlines formed in the urban East, Congress again began consideration of bankruptcy legislation. But the terms of the bill, particularly as they applied to voluntary bankruptcy, could not be agreed on; and despite the pressing need for it, no bankruptcy legislation was even considered on the floor of the House or Senate for three years.

The Civil War increased the nation's commercial anguish. Northern merchants, owed an estimated $300 million by the South, saw this indebtedness cancelled out with the advent of the war. Insolvency became the order of the day, yet Congress, with the problems of war pressing down, could find no time to enact bankruptcy legislation.

Action on the bill was also stifled by a vehement disagreement on the subject of state exemptions. Should such exemptions be preserved under the federal act or should they be disallowed? One view had it that since the state exemptions were not uniform, they were in effect discriminatory; they favored the debtors of some states more than those of others. It was argued that Congress could not pass a law so "non-uniform" in its application.

Congress did not take serious action on a bankruptcy measure until 1864. That year Representative Thomas A. Jenckes of Rhode Island introduced legislation in the House, and he pleaded eloquently for its passage. "Never was there an occasion when the passage of such a law was so necessary, nor the demand so great," he said. "Thousands were wrecked in the Panic of 1857 who have never regained a firm foothold in any business. Thousands more were stranded in the repudiation of Southern debtors in 1860."

The bill was successful in the House, but the Senate did not act on it. Commercial interests in the North could see no value in any bankruptcy legislation until the war had been brought to an end and reconstruction begun in the South, and they were able to influence the Senate into postponing action.

The war ended in 1865, and the following year the Jenckes bill was again introduced in the House. It provided for voluntary or involuntary proceedings for all persons, and it included several compromise conditions regarding discharge. The act stated that one of three conditions had to be present before a discharge could be granted: consent of a majority of the creditors by the amount owed; consent of a majority of creditors by number, or a dividend available amounting to 50 percent or more of the claims. The bill passed in the House. For a time it was tabled in the Senate, but ultimately it was brought to a vote. Now there was strong pressure for passage from Northern interest who saw in the measure some chance of collecting at least part of those claims they held against Southern debtors. This support was an important factor in the bill's passage. The vote was 22 to 20. Thus, twenty-five years after the repeal of previous legislation, the country had a bankruptcy law—the Bankruptcy Act of 1867.

The new law did allow state exemptions, but in some instances its application was academic in this regard. It preserved those exemptions that existed in 1864, but that was a year when many states were not even in the Union, and their individual constitutions and laws had no relevance to the bankruptcy law. After the war the Southern and Western states adopted new constitutions and statutes providing for new exemptions, in most cases substantially increased in number and amount. In 1872 Congress amended the Bankruptcy Act of 1867 by adopting a provision that in all bankruptcy proceedings the state exemptions in force in 1871 should be made to apply.

In general, the Bankruptcy Act of 1867 was a dismal failure. The consent provisions necessary for discharge encouraged collusion between debtor and creditor. Under-the-table payments to creditors to gain their permission for a discharge were not uncommon. The law was also abused by debtors who allowed bogus claims, either in number or amount, to be filed against them, with the holders of these claims then voting for discharge.

Creditors used the law to enforce harsh and unnecessary liquidations. Legal insolvency at the time was defined as one's inability to pay an obligation or obligations as they fell due. A creditor might hold a claim of as little as $250 against a debtor, but if the debtor found himself temporarily without the money to repay, the creditor could thrust the debtor into involuntary bankruptcy at once.

The act grew brutally oppressive in the way it was administered, too. This was particularly true in the South, where carpetbagger judges were found guilty of fraud, corruption and the misapplication of funds in their administration of bankruptcy proceedings. But everywhere, not alone in the South, fees to court officials grew increasingly excessive, absorbing whatever assets existed. Dividends paid to creditors seldom exceeded 10 percent of the total claims. Creditors in every section of the country cried out against such injustices.

By January 1873 dissatisfaction with the Bankruptcy Act had become so universal that the House of Representatives could pass a bill for repeal without debate and with a two-thirds majority. The Senate did not take action on the measure, however.

The Panic of 1873 brought the manifold defects of the act into sharper focus. It was a time of currency inflation and credit inflation, of government waste, of overinvestment in railroads, factories and new construction. In 1872, a year before the panic, the country had suffered more than 4,000 business failures. What triggered the pandemonium was the failure of a number of important Eastern firms, including the New York Warehouse and Securities Company, Kenyon Cox and Company and, the final blow, Jay Cooke and Company. Congressmen charged that these failures had been hastened and even caused by the Bankruptcy Act.

President Grant, in his Special Message to Congress delivered on December 1, 1873, was in accord with this view and recommended the course of action he felt necessary. Said the President: "Those who otherwise might make lawful and just arrangements to relieve themselves found difficulties produced by the present stringency in money and prevented by their constant exposure to attach and disappointment by proceedings against them in bankruptcy, and besides, the law is made use of in many cases by obstinate creditors to frighten or force debtors in a compliance with their wishes and into acts of injustice to other creditors and to themselves. I recommend that so much of said act as provides for involuntary bankruptcy on account of suspension of payment be repealed."

The House quickly followed the President's recommendation—in fact, it did more. On December 16, 1873, a bill calling for the full repeal of the act was carried 219 to 44 after only two hours' debate. The Senate was less impetuous, however. Instead of repealing the measure, it amended it.

One change had to do with the consent conditions concerning the discharge. The Senate adopted a provision (and later it was affirmed by the House) that no one could be adjudged a bankrupt unless one quarter of the creditors in number, or one third in amount, gave consent to the action.

More important, the Senate provided that the principles of composition and extension were to be made a part of the law, following a precedent set by England's Bankruptcy Act of 1869. To be wholly voluntary in their use, these principles allowed debtors to reorganize both their secured and unsecured debts and gave them an extended time for payment. When this feature of the act became law, it marked a significant turning point in bankruptcy legislation in the United States. No longer was the law to be concerned merely with the selling and distribution of the debtor's assets for benefit of his creditors and the release of the debtor from the burden of his obligations. Now bankruptcy law provided for the *rehabilitation* of the debtor. In the years that followed, the principles of composition and extension were recognized as being eminently constitutional by the Supreme Court. They serve as the essence of the present Chapter XIII of the act.

But the new provisions did little to stem the nation's contempt for the act as a whole. Debtors felt viciously oppressed by it; creditors felt that it ruthlessly exploited them through waste, fraud and irresponsible administration. Demand for repeal came from every quarter.

Senator James R. McCreary of Kentucky introduced repeal legislation in the Senate in April 1878. He called the act an "assault upon public morals in its violation of good faith in its craft, its falsehoods and frauds." The bill was adopted by the Senate after only two days of debate, and it was passed in the House in even less time. There the margin was overwhelming—205 to 40. Again the country was without national bankruptcy legislation.

Sporadic attempts to pass a new law were made during the 1880s, but they met with no success at all. The injustices of the Bankruptcy Act of 1867 caused such ill feeling toward bankruptcy in general that there were very few who would take a stand in favor of a law on the subject. As late as 1893, it was said in Congress, "The prejudices created by the abuses under the Act of 1867 make a fair discussion of any bankrupt act difficult."

When bankruptcy legislation was next enacted it was as a consequence of the Conventions of National Commercial Organizations held in St. Louis and Minneapolis in 1889. These businessmen, representing twenty-five states and territories and forty trade associations, wanted a law that would "permit the discharge of only honest men and visit condign punishment upon all who pervert its provisions to the achievement of selfish and fraudulent ends; and should be so formed as to allow proceedings in bankruptcy to be entered and prosecuted with the least possible expenses to the parties concerned, so that the sustenance of the debtor may not be frittered away in useless costs and other official charges."

A young St. Louis lawyer named Jay L. Torrey framed a bill which the conventions felt met these purposes, and it was introduced in the House, where it came to be known as the Torrey Bill, in 1890. The House passed the measure, but, as had been the case so often in the past, the Senate did not act on it. The foremost opposition came from Southern Senators who felt that the bill represented the wishes of "rich and powerful commercial cooperations, wholesale dealers, boards of trade and associated jobbers."

The Panic of 1893 cooled Congressional enthusiasm for the Torrey Bill. When the depression struck, banks in the South and the West became hard pressed and hundreds closed, at least temporarily. Commercial failures were numbered in the thousands. All currency was at a high premium. With such conditions prevailing, Southern and Western Senators wanted no part of legislation that would make bankruptcy compulsory —involuntary—for any of their beleaguered constituents.

Congress' struggle with the Torrey Bill continued through most of the decade. At length, in February 1898, the bill did pass in the Senate and, the following June, in the House. President McKinley signed it into law on July 1, 1898.

The Bankruptcy Act of 1898 was a comprehensive legislative summary of what had preceded. It provided for voluntary and involuntary bankruptcy for all classes of individuals and corporations. It declared that state exemptions concerning a debtor's property must be preserved, and it enunciated the principle of consolidation. In 1903, 1909 and again in 1910, attempts were made to repeal the law, with Southern legislators spearheading the action, but the bids for repeal were unsuccessful.

The law received substantial use and by an increasing number of people. During 1905 approximately 12,000 people filed petitions. The number climbed to about 70,000 for the year 1935. The administrative machinery was not equipped to handle the increased workload, and serious mismanagement was the result.

Investigations were frequent. There was the Donovan investigation in 1929, the Thacher investigation in 1930–1931, the McAdoo investigation in 1933–1935 and the Jackson investigation in 1936. In 1939 Attorney General Frank Murphy felt compelled to appoint an eleven-man committee under Francis M. Shea to investigate alleged improprieties. It brought to light instances of waste, fraud and gross injustice on the part of referees, trustees, lawyers and judges. Though a vast majority of the supervisory officials were honest, sincere and dedicated individuals, the final report was highly critical.

It declared: "The present system of supervision and coordination does not work. There are far too many illegal acts; far too much unjustified expense, both with respect to the running of the system and with respect to the administration of individual cases; far too much unwarranted delay; far less confidence in bankruptcy than it could, and can, have."

The report, known as the Shea report, was published in 1941. After World War II—in 1946—Congress acted on it, amending the existing legislation with the passage of the Referees' Salary Act. This served to increase the administrative efficiency of the bankruptcy system a hundredfold. Definitions were clarified and conflicting sections of the act revised. Sections that related to preferences and fraudulent conveyances were tightened, and the jurisdiction of the bankruptcy court was expanded.

The Referees' Salary Act created a Division of Bankruptcy within the Administrative Office of the United States Courts which was charged with the responsibility to investigate complaints about bankruptcy administration, to examine the performance of the referees and to collect and disseminate bankruptcy statistics.

Many of the abuses under the former system of administration stemmed from the fact that referees were paid on a fee basis, the amount dependent on the assets the referee was able to find and distribute to the creditors. But with the Referees' Salary Act, a Referees' Salary and Expense Fund was established, to be funded from fees gained from bankruptcy filings and from petitioners' assets. Out of this fund referees are paid salaries of up to $20,000 annually. Referees are appointed for a six-year term by the appropriate federal judge and reappointed as necessary.

Bankruptcy administration continues to be a subject of careful scrutiny. Late in 1965 the Brookings Institution, a nonprofit research and education institution in Washington, D.C., under a grant of $314,000 from the Ford Foundation, launched a comprehensive study of bankruptcy problems in the United States. Described as "a fresh look at institutions, procedures, causes and results of bankruptcy, and related phenomena in the United States," the study was to be completed in 1968.

Since 1898, the year the present Bankruptcy Act became law, the act has been amended more than ninety times. The most comprehensive changes that took place came in 1938, partly as a result of the stock-market break in 1929 and the years of depression that followed. That period found many *non-business* debtors in deep financial distress and unable to pay their debts. To help relieve this situation, Congress created Chapter XIII, and thus instituted a method by which a wage-earner debtor could pay his creditors out of future earnings. The provision has been employed on only a limited basis, however.

The evolution of bankruptcy legislation, while sporadic, has been sweeping. Provisions that stirred vigorous debate in the House and Senate no more than a generation ago cause not the slightest controversy today. No longer does anyone question the constitutionality of the principle of discharge, in either voluntary or involuntary proceedings. It is duly accepted that bankruptcy applies to all individuals, not to just "merchants and traders." The principle of preserving state exemptions in bankruptcy proceedings is taken for granted and so is the principle of consolidation.

This is not to imply that today the subject of bankruptcy is legislatively tranquil. Not by any means. The nation's credit grantors, their nervousness increasing in proportion to the number of bankruptcies, have called for new changes in the law, and Congress is responding. The most significant of these would deny a discharge to the petitioner who is adjudged to have "the ability to pay." In effect, the measure would give the referee the right to "screen out" what has been termed "unnecessary" bankruptcy cases. Thus, as in days past, the principle of discharge may become a conditioned one. Another proposal would allow courts of bankruptcy (in preference to state courts) to determine what debts are dischargeable and what ones are not in any given case.

Today, as has always been the case, the Bankruptcy Act has its critics. They claim that much of what is now happening under the provisions of the law would be abhorrent to the framers of the Constitution, and that the constitutional grant ". . . to establish uniform laws on the subject of bankruptcies throughout the United States," has been wholly tyrannized. In 1822 Ralph Lockwood, a writer of the period, best distilled this viewpoint when, in light of bankruptcy legislation then being proposed, he declared that the Constitution is "a nose of wax in the hands of some gentlemen who can always make it just what fashion pleases them."

But the founders were purposefully not specific as to the future application of the law. In an insolvency case in the U.S. Supreme Court in 1875, Mr. Justice Miller expressed this side of the debate in convincing terms: "They were not," he said, "building a strait-jacket to restrain the growth and shackle the spirits of their descendants; they were devising a political instrument, while firm, was nevertheless to be flexible enough to serve the varying needs of a changing generation."

CHAPTER 4

STRAIGHT BANKRUPTCY

To the cognoscenti, bankruptcy is known as "taking a bath" or "going through the wringer." Or a bankrupt person may explain to a friend that he "crashed and burned." A Chicago lawyer calls it "the great national cop-out." But the classical definition of bankruptcy is that it is ". . . a law for the benefit and relief of creditors and their debtors, in cases which the latter are unable or unwilling to pay their debts."

Bankruptcy works to the benefit of creditors by providing for the distribution of the debtor's assets among them. It works to the benefit of the debtor in that it grants him a discharge, a legal release from what he owes. This system is known as "straight" bankruptcy. During 1967, 85 percent of all non-business filings were of this type. Proceedings in straight bankruptcy are contrasted to Chapter XIII filings, or wage earners' plans. In these, the debtor agrees to pay his debts out of future earnings and without any liquidation of his assets.

Besides a release from his indebtedness, straight bankruptcy offers the debtor a number of other substantial benefits. For one, it provides quick relief. Collection harassment may end the very day his petition is filed. In most cases, the relief is permanent; it lasts a lifetime, in fact. And straight bankruptcy is not unduly complicated. The whole procedure, from filing to discharge, may take less than sixty days.

The procedure that must be followed in filing a petition of bankruptcy is outlined under Chapters I through VII of the National Bankruptcy Act. (Chapter VIII of the act concerns the reorganization of railroads; Chapter IX, the debts of municipalities; Chapter X, the reorganization of corporations; Chapter XI, the modification or extension of corporate indebtedness; Chapter XII, the composition of debts by persons other than corporations; and Chapter XIV, U.S. Maritime Commission liens.) Any "natural person," says the Bankruptcy Act, may file a petition of bankruptcy, with mere insolvency providing the basis for the filing. A person is deemed to be insolvent whenever the aggregate of his property shall not at fair valuation be sufficient to pay his debts. To put it another way, anyone whose debts are at least $1 more than his assets may file a bankruptcy petition.

Where does one file? In United States District Court. There are eighty-nine such districts, at least one in each state. Courts are usually located in the principal city or cities of the district, but sometimes they are especially scheduled into outlying areas.

When filing, a person may make a choice of districts. He is allowed to file in the district where he has his principal place of business, or in the district where he resides. A person living in Nassau County in New York State but operating a business in New York City could file in either the Eastern District of New York, which embraces Nassau County, or the Southern District, which includes New York City.

Every petition in bankruptcy is referred by a judge to a referee. He takes testimony from both sides—the debtor and his creditors, that is—studies it and reports his judgment. An appointee and a deputy of the federal judges in the district, the referee has all the powers of a judge except the right to punish for contempt of court. He administers oaths to and examines witnesses, and he can order them to produce books and records he deems important to the hearing. He can grant, deny or even revoke a petitioner's discharge. The referee remains in charge of the case until it is concluded.

Originally a referee in bankruptcy was a mere assistant to the U.S. district judge, without any decision-making powers. But as the number of bankruptcies increased and the administrative system grew, the district judge came to rely on the referee more and more. In mid-1967 there were 215 referee positions authorized.

Almost every bankruptcy case begins when the debtor, under the great crush of the money he owes, seeks out a lawyer. There is no statutory requirement that one must engage a lawyer to file a bankruptcy petition, and a few people do not. However, the legal forms necessary to filing, while available at most legal stationers, are quite formidable and are likely to perplex the average person.

A lawyer's services are of real value. He provides intelligent counsel, appraising the debtor's financial condition and surveying the alternatives he may have. He advises the debtor what assets he is entitled to keep and what debts he may still have once he has received his discharge. Once the petition has been filed, the lawyer explains the court procedure that is to ensue. The lawyer represents the bankrupt at the first meeting of creditors and is, in general, the bankrupt's liaison with the court and the creditors, or the trustee.

Lawyers' fees vary. In New York City a lawyer may charge $300 for handling a bankruptcy case. In many areas of the country the fee is $200 for an individual and $300 for a husband and wife.

Once it has been decided that straight bankruptcy is the only possible course, the lawyer usually asks the debtor to complete a work sheet. On this the debtor lists such information as his employer, his wages, his assets and his debts. For each debt, he gives the name and address of the creditor, the amount owed, and he notes whether the debt is secured and, if it is, he tells what the security is.

The first formal step is the filing of a "Voluntary Petition in the Bankruptcy of an Individual." It is a petition in the strictest sense of the word. "Your petitioner," states the petition, "owes debts and is willing to surrender all his property for the benefit of his creditors . . ." It concludes with this statement: "Wherefore, your petitioner prays that he may be adjudged by the court to be a bankrupt within the purview of said Act."

Besides the petition, the debtor also files a schedule of his debts and assets and a Statement of Affairs. Each has to be executed in triplicate.

The filing fee, paid to the clerk of the court, is $50. This is apportioned among the Referees' Salary Fund, the Referees' Expense Fund, the clerk and the trustee, if one is appointed.

If the petitioner is unable to pay the filing fee in full, the court will allow him to pay it in installments. Sometimes lawyers also make this arrangement concerning their fees.

The listing of debts must include all secured and unsecured claims, taxes, dues, notes, bills—everything. Failure to list any one of them is considered a false oath, a breach of the law. The petitioner has to be just as scrupulous in setting down whatever he owns or is owed to him, regardless of its value. He must list the cash he has on hand and the amount of money he has in the bank. He must list real estate, negotiable and non-negotiable securities, insurance policies, household furniture, automobiles and other vehicles, machinery and tools and all other personal property. A jeweler would list his watch-making equipment. A farmer would list his horses, cows and other farm animals and all his farm implements.

In his Statement of Affairs, which is prepared in question-and-answer form, the debtor supplies information about his occupation, income, tax returns, bank accounts, safe-deposit boxes, property held in trust, any losses he may have incurred through theft, fire or gambling, and any legal action in which he might be participating, either as a plaintiff or a defendant. One question refers to loan payments that the petitioner may have made in the year preceding his filing. His answer has to include the name and address of the lender, the date and the amount of the loan, and must define the debtor's relationship with the lender, specifying whether he was a partner, a business associate, a relative or a friend.

As soon as the petition is filed, the debtor is declared a bankrupt and his creditors are notified of that fact. They are requested to file their claims. Most do. If this is not done, they cannot share in dividends that might result from the liquidation of the bankrupt's assets.

With the filing, the lawyer for the bankrupt is able to bring to a halt whatever legal action creditors have undertaken in their efforts to collect. He can put an end to a garnishment, for instance. One debtor had failed to pay his electric bill and his power was turned off. His attorney got it switched back on.

Not long after the petition is filed, the referee calls a first meeting of creditors. At this meeting the bankrupt is questioned as to the items contained in his listing of debts and assets and his Statement of Affairs. All of the bankrupt's creditors have an opportunity to examine him.

If there are assets available for distribution, the creditors have the right to elect a trustee. Usually a lawyer, the trustee takes title to the bankrupt's property.

The trustee is an officer of the court responsible to the referee for the liquidation of the bankrupt's estate in accordance with law. It is usual for him to meet with the bankrupt a few days after the first meeting to examine the bankrupt's assets and property in an effort to determine what precisely is available for distribution. He is empowered to convert the bankrupt's property into cash and to pay whatever dividends are declared by the referee. He must account to the creditors for all money received and expended. He may petition the court for permission to appoint a lawyer and an accountant, setting forth justification. The trustee and his two appointees are paid out of the assets before any general distribution is made.

The first meeting, and all subsequent meetings, are held in federal district court and in a room which has all the appurtenances of a courtroom. The referee presides as a judge and the proceedings resemble a trial, although they are somewhat less formal.

In the years prior to the Chandler Act, which was passed in 1938, the bankrupt was not required to appear in court for examination. Even if he did appear, he was not usually examined by his creditors. Today it is different. The Chandler Act provided that "The judge or referee shall preside and . . . shall publicly examine a bankrupt or cause him to be examined and permit creditors to examine him."

Such examinations vary widely in character. What transpires depends on the amount of indebtedness involved and whether there are any assets. They also depend on the referee and the manner in which it is usual for him to conduct hearings.

The first meeting usually begins with the swearing in of the bankrupt by the referee. Then the lawyer for the bankrupt begins an examination of his client. It is rather *pro forma*. He begins by asking the bankrupt to state his name, address and occupation. "Have you read and studied these schedules?" he asks, presenting the debt and address listing. "Do they contain a true and complete statement of your assets and liabilities?" he asks.

The referee often asks the bankrupt if all of his creditors

have been listed. Sometimes he seeks to determine what precipitated the petitioner's financial tangle.

Then the referee asks if any creditors—or the trustee, if one has been appointed—wish to examine the petitioner. Surprisingly, few, if any, creditors attend bankruptcy proceedings. Therefore, it is not unusual for the first meeting to be the only formal meeting. Sometimes it lasts only a few minutes, and in some district courts as many as fifteen petitioners may be examined in a single morning session.

The bankrupt is always under oath when being examined, and any false statement constitutes perjury. This, or evasive answers, including the statement "I don't remember" when the petitioner is questioned about a fact that should be obvious, can cause him to be cited for contempt of court. The referee has no power to punish for contempt, but he must refer the matter to district court. Here the bankrupt is usually allowed to purge himself of the charge by complying with the order. He risks imprisonment by not complying. A false or evasive answer can also serve as a basis for an objection to the discharge being sought.

Referees have no sympathy for the petitioner who tries to hold out assets by a refusal to produce account books. In the Southern District of New York one bankrupt told this tale of woe: "I was riding on the subway on the way to see my lawyer. I had my ledgers in my briefcase at my feet. I fell asleep and didn't wake up until the train pulled into my station. I jumped up and got off in a hurry, forgetting the briefcase. When I realized what I had done, the train had pulled out and my books were gone forever."

The referee was unimpressed. He authorized turn-over proceedings to compel the petitioner to produce his records. Eventually he did.

Race-track losses and robberies are standard alibis used by

petitioners to explain the evaporation of large amounts of cash. But some people are creative in their defense. One debtor, asked to explain how $5,000 seemingly melted away, reeled off this account: "I love money so much that I always carried that $5,000—in five bills—under the strap of my wrist watch. One Friday night I lit the candles on the living-room table and spread out the money so I could admire it. It was windy and the flames set the bills on fire. They burned while I yelled for help."

Though impressed by the petitioner's inventiveness, the skeptical referee instituted turn-over proceedings. The $5,000 came to light in a bank account under the name of the debtor's wife.

Whenever the bankrupt is examined he is entitled to have his lawyer present, and the lawyer has the right to object to questions he considers not to be in accordance with established rules. The Bankruptcy Act provides that testimony cannot be self-incriminatory. It states: "No testimony given by him [the petitioner] shall be offered in evidence against him in any criminal proceeding, except such testimony." This immunity has been held insufficient in certain circumstances, however.

In cases where there are assets available for distribution, the law prescribes which creditors are to be paid first. Costs of administration—that is, the trustee's fee and expenses—are pre-eminent. Taxes, debts for wages and certain other liabilities have priority claim, too.

However, under no circumstances can the court destroy the value of the secured creditor's *security*. If the bankrupt has an equity in the mortgaged property, then the trustee sells it but must pay off the secured creditor. Only the money above the value of the security goes into the estate of the bankrupt. If the trustee feels the bankrupt has no equity in the secured property, then the trustee abandons it and the secured creditor can reclaim the property.

Sometimes a secured creditor will repossess his collateral and then, if a balance still exists, file a deficiency balance. This puts him in the same category with the general creditors. They are the last to be paid.

Under the terms of Section 6 of the Bankruptcy Act, the petitioner is allowed to keep certain goods as prescribed by the law of his state. These exemptions apply to both homesteads and personal property, and they cover a wide range.

California's exemption statutes are among the most liberal of any state. They allow the bankrupt to keep a house in which he has up to $15,000 in equity. He can also keep $1,000 in the stock of a savings-and-loan association, all his furniture, including a radio and a television set, and fuel enough for three months to keep his house warm. He may also retain money that he has in a pension or retirement fund; he can keep a cemetery lot and a car, the value of which cannot exceed $300, however. A tradesman may keep his tools, a professional man may keep his library and an entertainer may keep his wardrobe. More than one actress has been allowed to keep her expensive mink coat because the referee deemed it to be an important part of her wardrobe.

While California is charitable toward the bankrupt, many states are not. In eight jurisdictions—Connecticut, Delaware, District of Columbia, Indiana, Maryland, Pennsylvania and Rhode Island—there is no homestead law—that is, the debtor's home is not exempt from seizure. In other states the homestead exemption ranges from $1,000—the figure in Maine, New York, North Carolina and Ohio—to an unlimited dollar value, which is the case in Florida.

The personal-property exemptions vary just as drastically and often cover a list of bizarre items. They reflect the fact that most exemption statutes are frightfully obsolete.

Alaska exempts "one yoke of oxen, or a span of horses or mules, or two reindeer, or six dogs, as the case may be." In

Idaho, state law puts exemptions on ". . . the cabin of a miner . . . sluices, tools, pipes . . . one saddle animal . . ." Mississippi allows the petitioner to retain "the agricultural implements of a farmer necessary for two male laborers; two head of cows and calves, ten head of hogs, twenty sheep and goats each, all poultry, and all colts under three years raised in the state . . ." Many states allow petitioners to keep "a seat or a pew in a place of public worship."

California's lenient exemption statutes are believed to be one of the reasons that the state ranks seventh in the number of bankruptcies per capita. Said a Los Angeles bankruptcy referee: "A person here can go through bankruptcy and still come out with $20,000 or $30,000 worth of property, including an automobile, television, a homesteaded house, appliances and clothing." Indeed, when one "starts over" in California, he begins at a rather high level. However, in the great majority of filings state exemption laws are of small consequence, even in California, and for very good reason: Most petitioners own nothing or practically nothing.

In a final meeting of creditors the trustee accounts to the court and the creditors, reporting what funds he has collected and distributed. The bankrupt may or may not attend the final meeting.

In the normal no-asset case all of the proceedings, from the filing to the granting of the discharge, may take only two months or even less. However, in cases where there are assets available for distribution, the case may last six months or longer. And if, in addition, there are objections filed in an effort to prevent the discharge from being granted, the proceedings can be strung out for a year or more.

CHAPTER **5**

WHAT IT
ACHIEVES

The ultimate aim of every person who files a bankruptcy petition is to become wholly absolved from his financial obligations. This is done when the court issues a legal release called a discharge. In the great majority of cases it is granted in a routine manner.

Many people feel that a discharge frees the petitioner from any and all debt. Nothing could be farther from the truth.

The Bankruptcy Act states that "provable debts" can be discharged. A provable debt is one owed at the time of filing, and it is defined as "a fixed liability, as evidenced by a judgment or an instrument in writing."

However, not *all* provable debts are dischargeable. Taxes, for instance. A debtor cannot be released from any federal tax claims, or from taxes levied by any state, county, district or municipality.

As they refer to the subject of bankruptcy, the nation's tax laws have been sternly criticized. Some people feel that it is unjust that the down-and-out debtor must continue to be oppressed for the payment of back taxes, that this policy stands as a serious roadblock to anyone who seeks to re-establish himself socially or economically. It has been proposed that the bankrupt be required to pay only those taxes incurred during the year prior to his filing (except in the case of false returns or failure to file a return). But tax authorities have resisted these proposals.

Not only do the federal government and other taxing authorities insist that they be paid; they demand to be paid first. The Internal Revenue Service has a pre-eminent claim on whatever assets the bankrupt might be able to show, and can shoulder aside private creditors to take all or any part of anything that has exchange value. Many people feel that the federal government—that no taxing authority for that matter —should have the right to exercise such priority.

There are other claims besides taxes that are not dischargeable. A judgment against the petitioner for "willful and malicious" injury to the person or property of another is not dischargeable, nor is a liability imposed for obtaining money or property under false pretenses. Alimony or maintenance and support payments cannot be discharged.

A petitioner will not be released from debts created by fraud, misappropriation or embezzlement. He will not be discharged from wages due an employee and earned within three months of the initiation of bankruptcy proceedings, nor money an employee may have deposited with him to secure the performance of an employment contract.

Money due "unscheduled creditors" will not be discharged. That is, if the petitioner fails to list a creditor on his schedule of debts, the claim is not removed. However, if the petitioner overlooks a creditor in preparing his list of debts and that creditor gains notice of the bankruptcy proceedings, his claim would be dismissed along with those of the listed creditors.

A petitioner can be refused a discharge if he is found guilty of any crime meant to defeat the Bankruptcy Act. Such criminal acts deal with the concealment of assets from the trustee or with the swearing of a false oath. They also refer to any false entry or the falsifying of any document relating to the proceedings, or bribery. In such instances, proof has to be submitted that shows that the petitioner acted knowingly and with intent to defraud. He is not likely to be held blamable for a bookkeeper's innocent mistake or an accountant's unintentional error or his own.

A discharge can be refused if the petitioner's records are unavailable or flagrantly disorganized. The referee must be able to determine the petitioner's financial condition and ascertain his business transactions. The petitioner must be able to explain adequately any losses of assets or any deficiency of assets to meet his liabilities.

A discharge can be refused if he is found guilty of attempting to conceal property or fraudulently transfer property in the year before the filing of his petition. Again, intent is important. It must be shown that the petitioner meant to deceive or conceal.

No discharge will be granted to any petitioner who has received a previous discharge within a six-year period.

Last, the petitioner must cooperate with the court and with the trustee throughout the proceedings. He must answer material questions and obey lawful orders.

Using one or more of the grounds cited above, any one of the petitioner's creditors or the trustee can file an objection to the discharge. Then the court fixes a time for a hearing on the objection. The person doing the objecting must prove a case against the petitioner. If such a case is made, then the burden shifts to the petitioner to prove his innocence.

There are cases of a discharge, once granted, being revoked. If, within one year of the granting of the discharge, any of the parties in interest are able to show that the bankrupt person committed fraud—that is, was guilty of false oaths or concealed or misrepresented facts—and the knowledge of such fraud became known after the discharge was granted, the discharge can be rescinded.

One point must be stressed concerning the discharge: It does not really cancel out one's indebtedness. What it does do is serve as defense against any creditor who might take legal steps to collect a debt.

Sometimes a person who has been granted a discharge is taken into state court by a creditor. It is often the case that the creditor is simply ignoring the discharge, and he realizes full well that his debt is provable and dischargeable. His motive is to coerce the bankrupt into paying through sheer harassment. Some small-loan companies are guilty of this.

In such instances, the referee in bankruptcy can be of no aid to the debtor, for once the case is closed the referee loses jurisdiction. He can regain jurisdiction only if the case is reopened, and this requires the payment of an additional $50 filing fee.

What can happen is that the bankrupt may fail to appear in court for the simple reason that he believes his discharge has rendered him debt-free. Or it has happened that the bankrupt failed to appear because he never received a summons. Sometimes he cannot afford to hire counsel. In any event, the result is that the creditor gets a judgment against the debtor.

In *Local Loan vs. Hunt,* a landmark case, the Supreme Court decided that a bankruptcy court had the power to enjoin a proceeding in state court that was based on a discharge. However, the bankruptcy court can exercise this jurisdiction only in unusual or compelling circumstances. Thus it is seldom used.

Sometimes the action that the creditor brings charges that the debt is not dischargeable because the bankrupt gave a materially false financial statement in applying for his loan or for credit. Since the creditor extended credit on the basis of the statement, he charges that he is the victim of fraud.

To solve these problems it has been proposed that the Bankruptcy Act be amended so as to authorize the bankruptcy court to determine whether any debt is dischargeable. So-called "dischargeability bills" have been pending before Congress for more than a decade.

It is doubtful whether this legislation, if passed, would do much to resolve the situation. Such legislation would do nothing to deprive the state courts of their jurisdiction. Therefore, a creditor could still bring a non-dischargeable-debt suit. Dual legal proceedings would be the result, and this situation would cause the debtor even greater travail than he now may be suffering.

Such legislation might also put an additional and enormous burden on bankruptcy referees, for each debt could become the subject of a separate hearing.

One solution might be to change the wording on the discharge. It now reads: "It is ordered that said John Smith be, and he hereby is, discharged from all debts and claims which, by the Act of Congress relating to Bankruptcy, are made provable against his estate, except which debts as are, by said Act, excepted from the operation of a discharge in bankruptcy." This is a bit misleading. The discharge is merely the bankrupt's defense against legal means of collection any one of his creditors might take. This should be stated on the discharge itself.

Historically, bankruptcy court has determined whether a petitioner has the right to a discharge. State courts have traditionally ruled on the effect of the discharge. Thus a system of checks and balances has been operative. There seems little reason to upset it.

Straight bankruptcy is not an infallible remedy. To the person who falls into debt beyond any hope of ever paying, it presents one overriding benefit: It wipes the slate clean. But straight bankruptcy is not without its drawbacks.

Foremost, of course, the bankrupt loses whatever assets he may have that are not exempt under state law. Sometimes this results in poignant losses. There have been cases of engagement rings and even stamp collections being turned over to a trustee for sale.

But there are more than financial considerations. There is still a stigma attached to straight bankruptcy. How much of a stigma depends on the circumstances. In most big cities almost any filing is taken with a shrug. Says a Chicago court official: "Going into bankruptcy here is about as scandalous as having a head cold." In Southern California bankruptcy has gained almost as much acceptance as the backyard swimming pool.

But in small cities and towns, bankruptcy for the individual can be a painful experience. To creditors the filing of a petition is clear notification that a promise to pay is not going to be kept. A filing used to be accompanied by such stinging shame that a family would move from the area where it was known. It is not that bad today. Nevertheless, the petitioner and his spouse are likely to notice that a freeze prevails at PTA meetings and church socials—any gathering, and not just from creditors but even from friends. Some people still have the feeling that the bankrupt has perpetrated a swindle and that he really has money some place.

Of course, the bankrupt's emotional make-up is a vital factor in how he reacts to his filing and discharge. To some people it is a crushing defeat, and it takes long years to recover. To others it represents a fresh start; it is a stimulus.

Another disadvantage is that the bankrupt is stamped a bad

credit risk by some credit grantors. This is somewhat academic, however. By the time the debtor files his petition, collection agencies usually have him under siege and he has fallen victim to suits and attachments. Thus the distinction in his credit rating before and after bankruptcy is light.

Banks and financial institutions that deal in large sums of money will seldom do business with a bankrupt person. It is doubtful whether he ever could obtain a mortgage on a home. Again, the circumstances are important. For instance, if a person's bankruptcy is precipitated by a court judgment rising out of a personal-injury accident, he might be regarded a better risk than someone who simply spent himself into insolvency.

A bankrupt person is not likely to encounter much difficulty in obtaining credit for ordinary purchases. And even when it comes to buying a refrigerator or an automobile on credit, the bankrupt usually has no problems—and for a very good reason. The seller merely obtains a chattel mortgage on the merchandise. His security is right to repossess.

There are some merchants who seek out bankrupts, urging them to make credit purchases. They realize that a person who has gone through bankruptcy cannot file again for six years. In this respect, his credit is good.

"We do not hold bankruptcy against a person's credit," proclaims a letter from a St. Louis furniture and appliance dealer to any person who files a petition in district court in that city. "I will personally see to it that credit is extended to you," the letter declares.

A Chicago clothing and jewelry store sends petitioners in that city a credit card and a $10 gift certificate. "Your account has been set up for $200 with no money down," an accompanying letter states. Some used-car dealers and small-loan companies use the same tack.

For many people, a reasonable alternative to straight bankruptcy would be to file a petition under Chapter XIII of the Bankruptcy Act. This sets up a plan under which a debtor pays what he owes over a period of time, usually three years. The court prohibits garnishment of wages and other claims. A trustee is appointed by the court to make certain that the debtor follows the plan. But few debtors know about Chapter XIII, and attorneys hardly ever recommend it. Despite the seeming advantages it offers, it is seldom used.

CHAPTER 6

CHAPTER XIII:
WHAT IT IS,
HOW IT WORKS

On March 19, 1967, a woman, whom we shall call Lillian Kuhn, a twenty-nine-year old Chicago divorcee, got out of debt for the first time since the day of her wedding nine years before. She did it by virtue of a little-known piece of federal social-service legislation called "Chapter XIII" of the National Bankruptcy Act of 1938.

After Lillian's marriage broke up she was left with almost $2,900 in debts. She owed a total of $2,000 to three finance companies, $350 in unpaid department-store accounts and $500 to a school that had offered her a correspondence course in typing and stenography. Her monthly take-home pay was scarcely sufficient to meet her mountain of obligations and provide an adequate home for herself and her small son.

Her creditors became hostile. Letters from creditors had a demanding tone and their constant telephone calls were a source of deep anxiety to her. A finance company threatened to go to Lillian's employer. That was the last straw. In desperation she fled to an attorney.

The lawyer suggested a Chapter XIII filing. He drew up a payment schedule for her to follow, filed it with the local district court along with a Chapter XIII petition, and then got her creditors to accept the plan. Every month Lillian turned over $90 to a trustee, a representative of her creditors who had been appointed by the court. The trustee deducted his fee and that of the referee, and the balance was paid to creditors. Once the filing took place, Lillian was relieved of the travail of collection pressure, including the threat of garnishment. It took three years for her to complete her payment schedule, but she has never had a single doubt that she did the right thing.

Lillian Kuhn's case is a typical one. Under the provisions of Chapter XIII, insolvent individuals or families pay off their debts under a court-supervised payment schedule. During fiscal 1967, 15.3 percent of all filings were of the Chapter XIII type—31,963 cases out of a total of 208,329.

For years Chapter XIII—sometimes called wage-earner bankruptcy—was looked on with skepticism in almost every federal court district. Even today opinion is divided as to its value. Many lawyers and referees prefer straight bankruptcy for their petitioners. Some lawyers aren't even aware that Chapter XIII exists. However, in a few districts the majority of cases of the Chapter XIII type—and in Alabama a whopping 81 percent of all filings—are under the provisions of Chapter XIII.

Chapter XIII is of fairly recent origin. When the Bankruptcy Act was framed in 1898, it had two basic purposes. It was meant to apply the property of an insolvent person to the payment of his debts, and it was also meant to relieve the honest and unfortunate debtor from his obligations, to give him a chance to start afresh.

In its specifics, the act was intended mainly to cope with

business failures. Consumer credit was virtually unheard of in 1898. Ours was an agriculturally oriented economy, and approximately 80 percent of the population lived on farms. Goods were often paid for in kind. For the normal sixty-hour work week, one earned about nine dollars. What credit did exist was only in the business and financial realm. It was not until after 1900 that consumer credit began to become an economic factor of any consequence.

At the same time that consumer credit was beginning its upward spiral, a change was being wrought in the type of person who was incurring debt. No longer was he self-employed or the owner of a business. More and more the average person's income was being derived from wages, salary or commissions.

The great depression of the 1930s brought these facts into sharp focus. When this new breed of working man was thrust into deep financial distress, each of his creditors found himself in an especially vulnerable position. Wage earners seldom owned property, and that meant there were no assets available for distribution.

In 1938 Congress took note of this situation of some alarm and enacted Chapter XIII. It was one of the many amendments to the act that were passed that year.

When Chapter XIII was first made law, its application was limited to those whose income did not exceed $3,600. In 1950 the limit was raised to $5,000, and in 1959 all monetary restrictions were eliminated. Now any wage earner may file a Chapter XIII petition.

Chapter XIII proceedings usually come about following a debtor's meeting with his lawyer. Judgments and wage garnishments, or the threat of them, are the usual reason a debtor seeks out an attorney. Then lawyers request the debtor to complete a work sheet in which he lists all his debts, assets and wages. From this, and based on such facts as the debtor's wages, rent and other absolutely necessary expenses, a payment plan is evolved.

Several factors are important at this stage. Proper attitude is one. The wage earner must resolve to buckle down, to work diligently to pay for his indebtedness. He must determine to halt all credit purchases. The consent and the cooperation of the debtor's spouse is vital, too. He or she must be fully aware that the plan will impose denial and sacrifice. Unless the married partners have this realization, the plan will not work.

Robert Ward, an Oakland, California, attorney who has specialized in Chapter XIII cases, in advising his clients on the implications of this type of filing, begins by asking them to liken their financial condition to a physical injury—a broken leg, for instance. "It's not going to get better until you have it treated," he says. "The cast for the broken leg can be compared to the payment plan under Chapter XIII. Each will take time to get used to. Each is going to restrict you from doing things you would want to do. But the 'injury' will mend, while without the cast it could only get worse."

The payment schedule, both to the amount and the period of time involved, must be altogether practical. The payments to creditors should amount to not more than 25 percent of the debtor's income. And the payment schedule should be for not more than thirty to thirty-six months. In cases where a greater percentage of income is pledged or a longer payment period is called for, the debtor is likely to develop a sense of futility toward what he is doing. As a result he grows remiss in meeting the payment schedule. Ultimately the plan fails.

Once the wage earner and his attorney have decided to follow the Chapter XIII course and have drafted a plan that they both feel is realistic, the next step is to file a petition. This testifies to the fact that the debtor is a wage earner, that he is insolvent and that he desires to effect a "composition," a

putting-together of his debts with an idea of paying a portion
of them at certain intervals, or an "extension," an extra period
of time for making payment, or both.

Along with the petition the wage earner (he is termed a
"debtor" in a Chapter XIII filing, not a "bankrupt") files a
schedule of his debts and assets, a listing of any contractual
obligations he may have and a Statement of Affairs. With the
filing of the petition the debtor is able to gain immediate relief
from garnishment and other forms of collection harassment. In
most cases interest on any claims against him ceases to accrue
with the beginning of proceedings.

The filing fee in a Chapter XIII case is $15, with another
$15 to be paid at the first meeting of creditors. It is possible
to file a Chapter XIII petition without prepaying a filing fee.
Instead, payment is provided for in the plan itself.

The debtor's payment plan is also filed with the court, and
it usually sets forth in detail how both secured and unsecured
creditors are to be dealt with. Creditors holding secured
claims, such as a mortgage on the debtor's home or a chattel
agreement involving an automobile or furniture, are dealt with
individually. One or more of these creditors may not wish to
be included in the plan, and in that case separate agreements
will have to be reached with each. The substance of these
agreements are filed right along with the plan.

Sometimes a secured creditor will repossess the mortgaged
property. Then he will file a claim for a deficiency judgment,
the difference between the amount owed and the amount for
which the creditor sold the property. This balance then becomes another unsecured claim.

If the debtor is unable to make payments sufficient to meet
the demands of both his secured and unsecured debts, then the
unsecured creditors have to wait until the secured creditors
are paid before they begin to receive payments.

Chapter XIII proceedings offer no protection for a co-signer.

In other words, a creditor may seek out the co-signer for payment despite the initiation of Chapter XIII procedure by the debtor.

Usually the court specifies that should the debtor incur indebtedness beyond the figure set by the court, the plan is automatically terminated. The protection of bankruptcy court is withdrawn, and the creditors can thereby resume whatever legal process they choose to enforce collection.

The plan takes into consideration that the debtor's circumstances may change, and provides for slight modifications. The court is empowered to increase or reduce the amount of any installment payment, or extend or shorten the time for making payments. Only the court may do this, it must be stressed. A debtor is never permitted to make arrangements with creditors other than those outlined in the plan.

The court sometimes makes allowances for the debtor who may have overlooked one or more small creditors, as happens quite frequently. It allows him to file an amended schedule, provided that the additional money due is not in excess of 10 percent of the total amount listed in the original schedule.

Occasionally the court provides that the debtor may begin payments before the plan is actually confirmed by the creditors and a referee appointed. There is good reason for this. It often happens that a considerable amount of time elapses between the filing of the petition and the acceptance of the plan by the creditors, through no fault of the debtor, creditors or court. It is simply normal judicial delay, and sometimes it can stretch to as much as six months or longer. The creditors, quite naturally, grow disgruntled as a result of the delay, and their dissatisfaction can jeopardize the plan's success. But if payment has begun, the confirmation of the plan by the creditors is more likely to be affirmed.

This provision also enables the debtor to make a clear demonstration of his good faith. He has stated that he wants to pay his debts, alloting a certain amount of his wages each month to do this. By beginning payment before the actual confirmation of the plan, he gives undeniable proof of his intent.

Once the plan has been drafted it is presented to each of the creditors. This is sometimes done by means of a "Circular Letter to Creditors" which advises them, first of all, that the debtor plans to file Chapter XIII proceedings and then details the payment schedule that the debtor proposes to follow. Each copy of the letter is accompanied by a "Creditor's Claim," which requests information confirming the debt, and a "Creditor's Acceptance of Plan" form, in which the claimant assents to the plan itself.

In order for the plan to become operable, a majority of the unsecured creditors, representing more than 50 percent of the money owed, must give their confirmation. Usually there is little difficulty in gaining the necessary acceptances. Most creditors are acutely aware that if the debtor is not permitted to file under the terms of Chapter XIII, he will simply file straight voluntary bankruptcy. In that event, the return to each creditor is likely to be nothing, or virtually nothing.

In cases where acceptances are not forthcoming it is usually because the creditors are not aware of just what Chapter XIII proceedings imply. Then it usually falls on the attorney for the debtor to meet individually with each of the creditors and explain the benefits to be gained by accepting the plan.

Sometimes a lawyer can prevail on one or more of the secured creditors to accept monthly payments that are less in amount than that set by the sales contract. In the Southern District of Ohio the court allows 6 percent annual interest on the balance owed secured creditors as an inducement to accept Chapter XIII plans.

After the plan is accepted by the creditors, the debtor's lawyer applies to the court for confirmation. If the referee is satisfied that the plan is feasible, that it is in the best interests of the creditors and that it has been proposed in good faith, he will confirm it.

In Chapter XIII proceedings, the creditors do not elect a trustee. There is usually a standing trustee appointed by the court. The trustee administers the plan, and one of the first things he does is set the method of payment.

The debtor may make his monthly payment directly to the trustee. The courts prefer, however, that the debtor's employer send each payment to the trustee, deducting it from the debtor's salary check. Sometimes the employer is requested to send the full amount of the debtor's pay check to the trustee. He then deducts the amount due under the terms of the plan and pays the balance to the employee. The trustee also makes whatever disbursements the plan calls for.

The matter of fees is a bit complicated. In straight voluntary bankruptcy proceedings the petitioner pays his attorney and the filing fees. Other costs are defrayed by the court (unless there are funds resulting from the liquidation of the bankrupt's assets). But in a Chapter XIII filing, the fee schedule is slightly different. Besides the filing fee of $15, the debtor must pay a referee's fee of $15. More important, he is also assessed a sum of up to 5 percent of the payments made by or for him. This goes to the trustee. He also may be assessed an additional 3 to 5 percent (depending on the district) for the trustee's expenses. Last, there is a court-system assessment of 1 percent.

Then there is the matter of the attorney's fee. Some areas use a set formula for establishing fees for attorneys in Chapter XIII cases. As an example, in Kansas the fee is fixed at 10 percent of the debtor's total scheduled indebtedness, or 50 percent of the deposits which are made by the debtor during the first six months of the plan's operation, whichever amount is the smaller. When such a formula is applied, however, there is a provision that the attorney's fees will not be less than $50 nor more than $200.

According to *The Business Lawyer,* Chapter XIII has worked best in those areas of the country where lawyers have been willing to accept a deferred-payment plan. For example, in Kansas, $50 of the lawyer's fees is paid as soon as funds are available. The balance is paid on a par with secured creditors. In other areas, 25 percent of the attorney's fee is paid in advance, 50 percent at the end of the first six months and the balance—25 percent—on the same basis as the unsecured creditors. Thus the attorney has a stake in the plan's success; his interest is assured over the three-year payment period.

Sometimes debts still remain at the end of the three-year payment period even though the petitioner has been faithful to the payment schedule. One of two courses is open to him concerning the balance. He can petition the court to have the payment period extended and continue payment, or he can apply to the court for a discharge. When he seeks to do this, the court schedules a hearing and, if the petitioner has just reasons for wanting a discharge and if there are no objections, the discharge is granted.

The court has no power to force a debtor to comply with the plan. If the debtor stops making payment, he is not held in contempt or liable to penalty. In the case of the careless debtor, the one who just stops paying, the case usually reverts to the point where it began, with creditors demanding their money and employing every legal means to collect. Straight bankruptcy is the usual outcome.

If the petitioner finds that he cannot meet his payment schedule because the amount of his indebtedness is too formidable, he can make application to reduce the amount of his payments. As a last resort, he can convert the plan to straight bankruptcy. However, he must be able to satisfy the court that his failure to meet the plan's stipulations was due to circumstances for which he could not justly be held accountable.

Upward of 50 percent of the petitioners carry out their repayment plans to the end. "I've found that 60 to 70 percent pay to near completion," says a Kansas City attorney who handles more than 300 Chapter XIII cases annually. "Some of the remaining 30 or 40 percent find it necessary to convert to straight bankruptcy after they are on the wage-earner plan for a time. This is usually due to sickness or loss of employment or some other compelling reason." A Portland, Oregon, referee reports that about 40 percent of the Chapter XIII filings in his district fail and are converted to straight bankruptcy.

When a Chapter XIII plan does fail and there is no accident or misfortune involving the petitioner, it is often because the plan was unrealistic in the first place. It may have been formulated by someone not knowledgeable in financial planning, or the petitioner may have failed to provide his attorney with complete information concerning his indebtedness.

Of course, Chapter XIII proceedings aren't recommended for every single debtor. Some people are so inundated with bills and installment payments that straight bankruptcy may be the only course. Chapter XIII is only suitable where the debt load is not excessive and where the debtor has sufficient earning capacity to be able to pay. A sixty-four-year-old man —owing $6,400, and who had five children ranging in age from three to eleven and who earned only $40 a week—came before the court of a Madison, Wisconsin, referee with a Chapter XIII petition. Mercifully, the referee suggested that some other strategy might be more suitable.

Some states provide that a person heavily in debt may go into receivership, a condition not unlike Chapter XIII bankruptcy. The debtor initiates receivership just as he does a bankruptcy proceeding. He files a petition with the court along with essential personal information concerning his job and his income as well as a statement of his debts and assets. But he also makes an assignment of all his future wages to the court. In turn, the court recommends how the wages are to be allocated. In the state of Michigan an unmarried man who petitions for receivership knows he will be allowed to retain only 40 percent of his income—his take-home pay—for living expenses and that the rest will be distributed to his creditors. A married man is allowed to keep 60 percent of his income under Michigan law.

When a person is in receivership his wages cannot be garnished, and it is to prevent garnishment that this course of action is often chosen. However, any property the debtor may own is still liable to repossession.

One of the flaws in receivership is that it teaches the debtor almost nothing about handling his finances because the schedule of payment is fixed by law. On the other hand, Chapter XIII proceedings impose on the debtor the duty of evolving a practical repayment plan.

Also, receivership has no flexibility to it. It does not take into consideration emergencies that may develop once the plan is launched. For instance, should the debtor be suddenly confronted with a major medical expense, he cannot petition the court to revise his plan. He must either pay or drop it completely.

Finally, receivership puts no control on the debtor; he can run up new bills at will. But the provisions of Chapter XIII put a check on injudicious spending.

There can be no doubt about it—Chapter XIII filings are of benefit to both creditors and debtors. Its foremost advantage is that it gives the debt-burdened wage earner relief from garnishment and other collection pressures and added time to pay his debts. The benefits to creditors are obvious. They get paid, at least in part. In fiscal year 1966 the 28,261 Chapter XIII petitioners returned approximately $26.5 million to their creditors.

Chapter XIII also provides good basic training in money management. Most debtors in dire straits are the victims of their own poor judgment. They have had little or no training in the handling of their pay checks. Straight bankruptcy does nothing to overcome this failing, but a Chapter XIII filing, by virtue of the payment schedule that the debtor works out with his lawyer, does impart training and discipline in the use of money. Referee Harold Bobier of the Eastern District of Michigan says that debtors have told him that after they had completed their payments they began banking a sum of money equal to the amount they had been paying into the plan. Some debtors learned to buy on a cash basis as a result of a Chapter XIII filing, Referee Bobier says.

Filing under the provisions of Chapter XIII does not have nearly such a devastating effect on one's credit as straight bankruptcy sometimes does. Merchants, finance companies and banks do not look so disfavorably on a Chapter XIII plan. When a credit application asks, "Have you ever been adjudged a bankrupt?" the debtor who has filed a petition under Chapter XIII is entitled to answer "No."

The same type of question is often asked on employment application forms. Thus a Chapter XIII filing can mean that a petitioner might be able to obtain a job that would be barred to someone who had received a discharge under straight voluntary bankruptcy.

There are some workaday advantages, too. Under the terms of the payment plan the wage earner enters into, installments on an automobile, say, can be provided for under a chattel mortgage or similar security instrument and substantially as spelled out in the original contract. This means that the creditor is not permitted to repossess the vehicle. However, in straight bankruptcy, if there is no equity in the property, the creditor may petition the bankruptcy court to release the security. And even if equity does exist, the trustee is permitted to sell the property, converting it into cash for the benefit of the creditors.

Another practical benefit of Chapter XIII is that it serves to protect the debtor against suits filed by those creditors who may hold non-dischargeable claims. He pays those obligations right along with others.

Many referees who endorse and encourage the use of Chapter XIII do so on philosophic grounds. They feel that it achieves the fundamental purposes of the Bankruptcy Act: It works to the benefit of the debtor, his creditors and the public good. Despite the many and fairly obvious benefits it offers, Chapter XIII receives only slight use, and it has become a highly controversial subject among bankruptcy lawyers and court officials.

CHAPTER **7**

CHAPTER XIII:
USE AND NON-USE

Very few people take advantage of the provisions of Chapter XIII of the National Bankruptcy Act—only about one petitioner in every six.

While the number of Chapter XIII filings shows a steady upward climb, the rate of increase is about the same as that of the total number of non-business bankruptcies. Statistics from the Administrative Office of the United States Courts illustrate:

FISCAL YEAR	TOTAL NON-BUSINESS FILINGS	TOTAL CHAPTER XIII FILINGS	PERCENT OF TOTAL
1961	131,402	19,723	15.0
1962	132,125	22,880	17.3
1963	139,191	24,329	17.4
1964	155,209	27,292	17.5
1965	163,413	28,027	17.1
1966	175,924	28,261	16.0
1967	191,729	31,963	16.6

Some observers attribute the increase in the number of Chapter XIII cases for fiscal 1967 to the impact of the

Supreme Court's decision in *Perry vs. Commerce Loan Co.*
The decision, rendered in March 1966, overruled the Sixth
Circuit Court of Appeals and held that a wage earner could
apply for and receive extension privileges under the provisions
of Chapter XIII, even though he had received a discharge in
a previous proceeding filed within six years. (The increase in
filings represented the backlog in cases which had accrued in
the fourteen months between the two decisions.)

When statistics concerning the use of Chapter XIII are examined on a state-by-state basis, they show an almost bizarre
lack of uniformity. Many federal court districts had no Chapter XIII filings at all for 1966, a typical year. These districts
included New Hampshire, Delaware, Western Pennsylvania,
Northern Mississippi, Eastern Texas and Eastern Oklahoma.
In half a dozen other districts—Wyoming, New York, Indiana,
Montana, Vermont and Connecticut—less than 1 percent of
the filings were of the Chapter XIII type. It is almost as if
Chapter XIII was not available in these areas.

In other federal districts, over the same period, the ratio
of Chapter XIII filings to all filings was startingly high. In
Kansas, 39.8 percent of all filings were Chapter XIII. Maine
showed 40.6 percent; Tennessee, 42.5 percent; Arkansas, 59
percent; and Alabama, 76.9 percent.

Why does this enormous disparity exist? Why do petitioners
in some districts show a preference for Chapter XIII while
those in other jurisdictions positively shun the statute? The
answer is not difficult to perceive. Chapter XIII is used
the most wherever its provisions are supported by local
referees, attorneys and creditors.

Quite often Chapter XIII is not utilized for the simple
reason that attorneys and petitioners are not aware that the
statute exists. What happened in the city of Flint, Michigan, is
a case in point. In 1963 Flint was a city in which virtually

every petitioner filed straight bankruptcy. Then Referee Harold H. Bobier launched an information program to boost the benefits of Chapter XIII filings. He prepared special pamphlets on the subject and delivered speeches before local credit unions, loan associations and bar associations in its praise. He urged attorneys to cite the values of Chapter XIII to their clients.

When he examined a petitioner in his court, Referee Bobier would determine if he knew of Chapter XIII and what it implied. In cases where the debtor was uninformed on the subject, Referee Bobier would adjourn the hearing to allow the petitioner and his lawyer to discuss the provisions of Chapter XIII and to permit the debtor to convert his petition to Chapter XIII. The result of this information program was an enormous upswing in the proportion of Chapter XIII filings in the Flint district, with an accompanying downtrend in straight bankruptcies.

Another reason for the infrequency of Chapter XIII filings is that attorneys feel that such proceedings are too complicated, that they demand additional time and labor with no commensurate increase in fee. Indeed in many areas this is true. One attorney, when submitting his client's petition to the court, asked that his $200 fee be given priority, "because I've already put $1,000 worth of work in on this." The referee granted the request, explaining that he didn't doubt that he had.

The costs involved in a Chapter XIII filing can also weigh heavily on the petitioner. The fees and expenses to the referee and trustee may be too much for him to bear. However, in some districts it has been possible to reduce fees substantially by increasing the efficiency of courtroom procedures.

Referee Herbert R. Maulitz of the Northern District of Alabama says that the "secret" to the very high percentage of Chapter XIII cases in his area is the "simplicity and convenience" that characterize every step of the procedure. ". . . we do everything we can to make it easy for the debtors' and creditors' attorneys, for creditors handling their own claims, and for employers of our wage earners," says Referee Maulitz. All necessary forms and documents have been simplified. Hearings are expedited. Employers are assured that their employees will not be harassed while their cases are pending.

Each large employer in the Birmingham area, the major city in the Northern Court District of Alabama, sends a single check to the bankruptcy court for the salaries of all his employees who are Chapter XIII petitioners. The court then mails a single check to major creditors in Birmingham, listing on an accompanying statement (prepared by IBM equipment) the names of the debtors and the accounts paid each. Members of the Birmingham bar charge only minimal fees when handling wage-earner plans.

As far as creditors in the Northern District of Alabama are concerned, the success of the program cannot be overstated. They receive about $4½ million annually in Chapter XIII disbursements.

The contrast between the number of Chapter XIII filings in Kansas City, Kansas, and Kansas City, Missouri, shows graphically how the administration of the statute can affect its rate of use. The two Kansas Citys have the same legal climate and are virtually a single economic unit, divided only by a street called "State Line." State laws concerning garnishment and with respect to interest rates and regulatory statutes concerning small-loan companies are almost identical in both Kansas and Missouri. Yet in 1966 the entire Western Court District of Missouri, which includes Kansas City, showed only 189 Chapter XIII filings out of a total number of 2,518 cases, while Kansas City, Kansas, had 1,321 Chapter XIII filings out of a total of 3,313 cases, a difference of 7½ percent to 39½ per-

cent. Claude Rice, a Kansas City, Kansas, attorney, says that
court officials in his city "honestly attempted to make Chapter
XIII effective." Debtors, their creditors and the local bar were
educated in the use of Chapter XIII. Automatic data-process-
ing equipment was installed to streamline accounting procedures. It provides a monthly automatic distribution of all
available funds in accordance with the provisions of each payment plan, and it automatically reviews each case to determine
whether or not the debtor is making his agreed-upon payments.
The equipment also prepares a final report for creditors when
the case is closed.

Cincinnati and the Southern District of Ohio is another area
where Chapter XIII has worked well. Its growing use there
dates to the year 1961. In June of that year the *Reader's Digest*
featured an article explaining the virtues of Chapter XIII.
It was entitled "Ready Help for People in Debt." As soon as
the article appeared, the district court began to receive in-
quiries about wage-earner filings. As a result court officials and
the legal profession were awakened to the provisions of the
chapter.

During 1962, 1963 and 1964, more than 1,900 people filed
Chapter XIII petitions in the Southern District of Ohio, and
by the end of 1964 more than 75 percent of the plans that had
been filed were still operative. The court had distributed more
than $1 million to creditors, and disbursements were continu-
ing at the rate of $70,000 a month.

William R. Schumacher, a Cincinnati attorney and a trustee
in local Chapter XIII filings, says that the successful use of
the chapter in his city has been due in part to the willingness
of several hundred employers to cooperate with the court by
sending debtor-employee's checks directly to the trustee or,
as an alternative, deducting the amount of the monthly payment from the employee's wages and forwarding it to the
trustee.

Chapter XIII, of course, remains unattractive to any debtor who might be caught up in a claim he regards as unscrupulous or unjust. To overcome this objection, proposals to amend Chapter XIII have been offered by Professor Vern Countryman, chairman of the Special Committee on Consumer Bankruptcy of the National Bankruptcy Conference. One proposal deals with exorbitant deficiency claims. It would authorize the bankruptcy court to determine the value of collateral and to allow a deficiency claim only in the amount by which the indebtedness exceeds the value, or the sale of the collateral, whichever one is greater. In some states, as it stands now, a creditor can repossess the merchandise, sell it, keep the money and still be entitled to whatever amount is due. Because of interest and fees, a debtor can wind up paying more for a piece of merchandise than it cost originally—and not have the merchandise. Any person who receives this type of treatment is not a likely candidate for a Chapter XIII filing. His inclination to pay is practically nil.

Another of Mr. Countryman's proposals has to do with unconscionable claims. It would authorize the court to refuse the enforcement of the remainder of any contract found to be unconscionable at the time it was executed.

Some people blame lawyers for the low number of Chapter XIII filings. "Most lawyers," says one referee, "know little about bankruptcy law, except that the petition for adjudication and discharge are vital to the procedure." Some, unskilled in family finance, make no distinction between the debtor who needs more time to pay his obligations and the one who is wholly unable to pay. The whole process is "too mechanical," says the referee.

The American Bar Association has censured some of its members for the infrequency of Chapter XIII findings. In a report issued early in 1966, the organization singled out for blame lawyers in New York City, Chicago, Southern California and northern Ohio. Too many lawyers in these areas simply advise individuals to file outright "grasshopper" bankruptcy petitions. The reason: lawyers get their fee quicker and have less work to do when filing a straight bankruptcy petition as opposed to a Chapter XIII case. Says Linn K. Twinem, chairman of the Consumer Bankruptcy Committee of the American Bar Association: ". . . some lawyers who have made a good thing out of personal bankruptcy . . . find it much more expedient and profitable to steer a debtor into straight bankruptcy rather than pursue the tedious course offered by Chapter XIII."

Mr. Twinem also blames some referees for their failure to make appropriate use of Chapter XIII. "Some of the older referees," he says, "appointed before the referees were dignified by a salary basis in 1946, are indifferent to the type of cases filed in their court and are not inclined to be burdened by the additional administrative details involved in processing a case through Chapter XIII."

As evidence presented earlier in this chapter indicates, in some jurisdictions referees recommend and even exhort debtors who come before them, or their attorneys or both, to give consideration to the provisions of Chapter XIII, rather than pursue a course of straight bankruptcy. As Mr. Twinem says, in some jurisdictions referees are indifferent. And in still others, referees oppose the urging of a Chapter XIII filing. They claim that such behavior is unbecoming. They point out that the referee in bankruptcy is under oath to administer justice, they feel, to urge an individual to consider the use of Chapter XIII.

To put pressure on a petitioner's attorney is just as unfitting. And some referees do this. They use psychological coercion and fear of judicial disfavor. Those opposed to this call it "judicial malpractice."

Adherents of Chapter XIII filings proclaim that straight bankruptcy is "a cancer that eats away at the moral fiber of the country." One referee who heard that statement shrugged his shoulders and said, "Of course, I'm concerned about the country's 'moral fiber,' but it's not my job to prod the people who come before me to what is considered 'good' for the nation or 'good' for themselves. I'm not a social worker. I'm a judge. I'm supposed to administer justice according to the law. If someone comes before me and wants to file straight bankruptcy, and his lawyer wants him to so file, and the case meets all the requirements of the law, who am I to urge another course of action? I think it would be improper."

There has to be a middle course. Chapter XIII is a worthwhile alternative to straight bankruptcy. It has real value to a debtor so long as the payments are not such that they place him or his family under undue strain and the payment schedule is not so long as to be oppressive. The statute can be made to work. It requires the cooperation of referees, lawyers and creditors in each court district and, of course, the cooperation of the debtors. In most jurisdictions, this cooperation has been lacking. But one day it may be made virtually mandatory.

CHAPTER **8**

CHANGING
THE LAW

A young man, a recent arrival in Chicago, sat tensely in the oak-paneled bankruptcy court of Referee Stephen R. Chummers, petitioning for the release from $9,140 in indebtedness. When the referee scanned the list of debts, he noticed that the total included a figure of $3,000 which the young man had borrowed from college and educational funds to pay for his college education.

"Are you working for a doctorate?" the referee asked.

"No," said the young man, "it's a Master's."

Chummers reddened. Besides the cost of his education, the young man's debts included $426.79 owed on an automobile, $900 on furniture, $420.42 on a television set, and more than $1,000 in clothing bills. There were medical bills and rent. The young man had received a fine education and had seldom denied his wants. Now he wanted to repudiate all that he owed. The referee asked for an explanation.

"Well," said the young man, "it's just that I just moved, just got out of school and moved to Chicago, and I would like to get a fresh start. Things have been piling up."

"Don't you have any desire to pay off the money you've

94

borrowed to pay for your education and that got you your Master's degree?" Chummers asked.

The young man shrugged.

Chummers had no choice. Under the law the young man was eligible for a discharge, and he got it.

Later, Chummers said that the young man's creditors were agreeable to having him pay off his debts over a three-year period. "I tried to shame him into paying," Chummers said, "but he didn't like the idea."

Bankruptcy cases like this one are about as amusing to the nation's retailers as rainy weekends before Christmas, and they appall the country's moneylenders. Credit grantors feel that people typified by the young man who came before Referee Chummers—that is, petitioners "with the ability to pay," as they describe it—should not be granted a discharge unless it is under the provisions of a Chapter XIII filing. They would give the referee the power to "screen out" what they term "unnecessary bankruptcy cases."

Creditor groups, out of their alarm, have awakened Congress to this seeming loophole, and in recent years legislation has been introduced in both the Senate and the House to amend the Bankruptcy Act so as to deny a discharge to those petitioners who are adjudged to have the earning power to pay their debts. Such legislation has not been voted into law— yet. But the pressure is strong. The American Bankers Association and the American Bar Association are among the groups that favor it. One day the unrestricted right to a bankruptcy discharge may be abolished.

Late in 1964 (so late, in fact, that there was virtually no chance the bill would be passed) Representative Emanuel Celler of New York introduced a measure which read: "At the first meeting of creditors, the . . . referee shall . . . determine whether the bankrupt has shown that adequate relief cannot

be obtained under Chapter XIII of this Act. In the event that
the judge or referee shall determine that the bankrupt has
failed to make a strong showing, he should enter an order
vacating the adjudication and dismissing the bankruptcy proceedings." The bill never reached the House floor. The next
year, in the next session, the same measure was introduced
as H.R. 292 but was not reported out of committee either.

Early in 1965 Senator Albert Gore of Tennessee introduced
a bill that sought to authorize the bankruptcy court—i.e., the
referee—"when it appeared feasible and desirable," to order
the petitioner to proceed under the provisions of Chapter XIII.
In introducing the legislation, Senator Gore indicated that he
was doing this because of his concern over the rising number
of bankruptcies in his home state. In the fiscal year of 1940,
4,644 bankruptcy petitions were filed in Tennessee. In 1964,
the year before the Gore measure was introduced, 8,767 petitions were filed, an increase of almost 100 percent. Ninety-
seven percent of the petitions were of the non-business type.
The Senator declared that the Bankruptcy Act had a "loophole by which anyone can shirk his duty to his community."

"Too many individuals," he stated, "who have good incomes
but few tangible, unmortgaged assets deliberately run up large
debts and proceed to file a petition in bankruptcy." The Gore
measure was never voted on.

Early in 1967 Representative Richard Poff, a Virginia
Republican, introduced in the 90th Congress a bill (H.R.
1057) identical to that of Representative Celler. Congress-
man Poff said that his amendment would encourage and
stimulate the use of Chapter XIII "in those instances where
it reasonably appears that a debtor could pay his obligations
out of future earnings without causing undue hardship." He
also pointed out that "responsible judicial, business, civic and
church leaders have long been concerned over the demoraliz-
ing and detrimental effects of avoidable bankruptcies."

Proponents of legislation that would "screen out unnecessary bankruptcies" cite four university studies which state that 25 to 50 percent of all personal bankrupts could have paid their debts over a period of time—usually three years—if they had been disposed to. Foremost of these is the study of 172 cases of straight voluntary bankruptcy in the Flint, Michigan, area conducted by Robert Dolphin, Jr., in 1963 and published by Michigan State University. The survey stated that 49 percent of the bankrupts could have paid off their indebtedness and still maintained an "adequate" income level. "Adequate" income was described as $2,763 annually, after taxes, for a family of four. And, according to Professor Dolphin, 28 percent of the 172 cases could have paid their debts while maintaining a "comfortable" standard of living. "Comfortable" was described as $3,600 annually, after taxes, for a family of four.

A study of bankrupts in the state of Utah, which was conducted by Grant L. Misbach in partial fulfillment of the requirements of a Master's degree at the University of Utah, set forth findings similar to those of Mr. Dolphin's. Mr. Misbach stated that "25 to 50 percent of the individuals who filed bankruptcy in Utah in 1963 were not hopelessly in debt and other solutions could have been possible without taking out bankruptcy."

Both the Dolphin and Misbach studies are a bit harsh on the debtor. To suggest, as Professor Dolphin does, that an income of $53 a week for a family of four is "adequate" is to be severe, indeed. And Mr. Misbach declares that when a family's debt payments are running as high as 50 percent of income, a repayment program is still possible. Perhaps.

If failings do exist in these studies, they are not serious ones. It is a matter of accepted fact that some bankruptcy cases are unnecessary and some are probably even tinged with fraud. Further, no one opposes the idea that a man with appropriate earning power should pay his just debts. But it is debatable whether legislation which gives the referee in bankruptcy the right summarily to deny a petition for straight bankruptcy is the way to solve the problem. Some observers typify such legislation as barbaric.

One objection to such legislation is that it would discriminate against the wage-earner debtor. In effect, it tells him he must meet certain payment conditions in order to obtain his discharge. But there are no similar conditions to be imposed on businesses. No referee is going to consider whether a corporation has the ability to pay when it seeks a discharge from its indebtedness.

Another objection is that such legislation would tend to make Chapter XIII filings involuntary. A wage-earner debtor, seeking relief from garnishment or other forms of collection but denied a discharge by a referee, would have Chapter XIII as his sole alternative. Yet one of the foremost requisites for the success of any Chapter XIII plan is the willingness of the petitioner to bear the burden of the payments. He has to have incentive. Anyone who has a payment plan thrust on him is likely to be lacking in desire. Even in voluntary Chapter XIII cases—that is, even when petitioners elect that course—not all successfully complete their payment schedules. In "involuntary" Chapter XIII cases, the proportion would be materially lower.

Many of the people who favor H.R. 1054 or similar legislation proclaim that today's debtor has a changed moral attitude toward indebtedness. Debtors no longer feel "a sacred obligation to pay." This may be true. But often the person who seeks to repudiate his debts feels in clear conscience he can do so. He may be the victim of unfair retailing tactics—high-pressure selling or an unconscionable installment contract. He may be struck with an exorbitant deficiency claim. In other words, morality is the business of both the buyer and the seller.

Bankruptcy referees already have considerable discretionary power. Some use it; others "go by the book." Nowhere is this more perceivable than in the administration of Chapter XIII. The statute is actually employed in only twelve states, and consider that in Alabama only one petitioner in six files straight bankruptcy; the other five come before the court as Chapter XIII petitioners.

In addition, Section 17 of the Bankruptcy Act specifies a wide array of debts from which the petitioner is not to be released. These include any liability incurred in "obtaining money or property by false pretense."

Seemingly, then, referees already have much of the power they require to refuse an unreasonable or unnecessary request for discharge. The problem seems to be in encouraging them to use this authority.

CHAPTER 9

THE CAUSES
OF BANKRUPTCY

What causes a bankruptcy? No one really has a clear-cut answer. The contributing factors are manifold and different in almost every case. They range from the inability to manage money to domestic problems and separation and divorce; from the aggressive collection methods that some creditors practice to a spell of just plain bad luck. Often it is an accumulation of causes rather than just one of them.

Let's establish some criteria first. Any individual's bankruptcy has both primary and secondary causes. A primary cause is a basic cause. An automobile accident that causes serious injury, then hospitalization and attendant and staggering bills is another.

Secondary causes are triggering causes. They are what push the debtor over the brink. A lawsuit instituted by a creditor is one example of a secondary cause. Garnishment, or the threat of it, is another. These are termed secondary causes because they do not actually create the situation in which the debtor finds himself; instead, they are the result of it. When you ask a petitioner why he is filing bankruptcy he will usually give you a secondary cause as his reason. He is likely to say, "To get that finance company off my back" or "Because I got some bad breaks." It is improbable that he will say that he lacks fiscal responsibility. No one likes to admit to any failing.

Few observers of the bankruptcy scene would argue with the statement that poor money management is a prime factor in almost every bankruptcy filing. There are many ways to define this: It is "Keeping up with the Joneses"; it is impulsive buying; it is failing to provide for emergencies. In sum, it is the failure to live within a budget, taking on only that amount of debt that one can handle. "I just got overloaded" is the way a bankrupt person is likely to describe the condition.

Professor Reed, in his study of 400 personal bankruptcy cases in the state of Oregon, declares that he did not encounter a single petitioner who operated on a family budget. "Most, if not all," he states, "were inept at money management. Indeed, financial planning was conspicuous by its absence, and it seemed as if petitioners lived from pay check to pay check."

Other studies bear out these findings. Dorie Jacobs analyzed 544 personal bankruptcy cases in the Southern District of Arizona in preparing her Master's thesis at the University of Arizona. Said Miss Jacobs: "These people buy! They purchase cars that are too expensive ever to be paid for. They buy color television sets, water softeners, stereo sets, and the records. Furniture is purchased which will long be worn out before it is paid for. They finance and refinance with illogical persistence."

The findings of Robert Dolphin, Jr., in a survey of 482 bankrupts in Genesee County, Michigan, also point up the lack of self-restraint of which many petitioners are guilty. In the year preceding their bankruptcy, 38 percent of those studied by Mr. Dolphin purchased jewelry, 40 percent bought furniture and appliances and 60 percent bought automobiles. "They not only accumulated more debt," said Mr. Dolphin, "but they used larger and larger amounts of debt each month as they approached the filing of their bankruptcy." They are like people pouring gasoline on a fire. A survey by Northwestern National Life Insurance Company concluded that the typical bankrupt owes twelve to eighteen creditors an average of almost one half of his income and is shoved into court by his own "incompetent financial management."

At its worst, credit buying can be as obsessive as gambling, narcotics or alcoholism. Dr. Milton H. Huber, associate professor at the Center for Consumer Affairs at the University of Wisconsin, in his study of 100 overextended families, declared that borrowing had become almost a conditioned reflex to them. "Their unswerving reaction to any new financial problem was to borrow more money," Dr. Huber states. Every family interviewed for the study had at least one consolidation loan and a significant number had three of them.

"For many people borrowing becomes a habit, almost like narcotics," says David Bell, an examiner for a Texas regulatory loan agency. "Some people are irresistibly attracted to loan offices, even when they may not really need to borrow."

A Texas attorney tells of one chronic borrower whose many creditors arranged for him to consolidate his various bills into a single and manageable loan of $1,600. The loan included a final payment of $7.50 on a watch that the man had purchased from a local jeweler. The man carried the $7.50 from the loan office to the store and paid the bill. But he wound up buying a camera for $200, on credit, before leaving the store.

Dr. M. R. Neifeld, for thirty-five years vice-president of the Beneficial Finance System, has characterized such people as "credit drunks." He says they are a "maladjusted type," and their maladjustment "manifests itself in compulsive debt involvement." They require psychiatric analysis and treatment, Dr. Neifeld states.

Why people buy with such inexorable compulsion and so little regard for their personal financial stability are questions that are beginning to trouble the nation's financial institutions and credit grantors. Two aspects of the problem stand out. First of all, bankrupts, for the most part, have an awful lack of knowledge and ability when it comes to handling money. They do not fully understand the meaning of four words: *asset, liability, income* and *expense.* They do not realize that income must be kept in balance with expenses, assets with liabilities.

The second and a convergent factor has to do with the enormous pressure on people nowadays to "buy now and pay later." As a result, people's attitude toward debt has undergone tremendous change. "Time has wiped away the Puritan connotation of immorality in debt and godliness in thrift" is the way *Newsweek* magazine put it. "Debt has been transformed from a stigma to status symbol, from a last resort of people in need to an entree to the good, material things in life." Indeed, this is the case. It is significant that the phrase "cash and carry" is no longer a part of our language.

The American advertising industry, while it has made a significant contribution to the high standard of living we enjoy, must bear some of the blame for this "new" morality. Our life is loaded with status symbols—the ranch-type home in the suburbs, the second car, the color television set, wall-to-wall carpeting and three weeks in Europe during the summer. These are the "good" things. To save and to wait to attain them is bad form. In some instances it is considered almost un-American.

"They dangle things in front of the public and talk about no money down and small monthly payments" is the way one person with a shaky financial situation put it. "They fool the average person into believing he can afford things he can't and that he needs things he doesn't need."

This is "easy credit," a situation that involves too aggressive selling combined with a lack of proper credit investigation and liberal credit terms. When a person asks a used-car salesman to quote a price on an automobile, a typical reply is "I can let you have it for $150 down and $62.40 a month for 36 months." The salesman avoids mentioning the total cash price or the interest rate on the contract. He knows that most people today can tell whether they can afford $62.40 a month much easier than they can tell if they can afford $2,200.

To some degree, the nation's department-store chains, discount operations, auto and appliance dealers are abusing the nation's credit system. As these outlets have multiplied in the last decade, so has their struggle for the consumer, and often their strategy takes the form of lenient credit practices. Many a merchant has opened a charge account for a person he knows to be deep in debt rather than lose him to a competitor down the street.

There are cases of used-car dealers being accused of selling cars to people who they know will have difficulty paying. When the payments do stop, the dealer simply repossesses the car and obtains a deficiency judgment for the balance due. Small-loan companies, often classed as the largest creditor of bankrupts in terms of money owed, have been blamed for their "hard sell" practices which tend to overload already heavily extended families.

It is generally believed that a person who has been declared a bankrupt will not be able to obtain credit again. This is no longer true. Some firms, principally banks and large lending institutions, have a policy of refusing credit to bankrupts, but there is a fairly widespread view among some retailers that a person who has been recently declared a bankrupt is not a bad credit risk. After all, he is likely to be relatively free of debt. Moreover, he is legally unable to file bankruptcy for another six years.

There is no doubt that easy credit is playing a significant role in the rising bankruptcy rate. And it seems logical to assume that if credit policies were made more rigid, the number of bankruptcies would decline. This may be true, but is it a solution that is generally desirable? Would it be fair to the 90 percent of the population that use credit judiciously? Instead, what seems to be required is a measure of self-control on the part of the buyer, some personal restraint. Or as William S. Naughton, Eastern Director of Industry Relations for the Seaboard Management Company, puts it, "To blame the credit grantor for the misuse or overuse of consumer credit is like blaming the automobile dealer for accidents."

Aggressive collection methods are often blamed for a great bulk of bankruptcies in any given year. Garnishment, the process by which a creditor can have part of a debtor's wages paid to him directly, is the foremost of these. A good number of bankruptcy referees feel that garnishment is the *prime* reason their courtrooms are crowded. Says Clive W. Bare, a Knoxville, Tennessee, referee, "Garnishment is the 'triggering' cause of bankruptcy. It drives many into bankruptcy who actually owe relatively small sums."

Having a portion of one's income cut off is serious business. But garnishment presents another and prevalent problem in that many employers look on such action as a reason for instant dismissal. Some employers have a policy of dismissing any employee who has his wages garnished a second time. A worker who has been threatened with garnishment often takes refuge in bankruptcy court. It's better than being fired, he feels. In other words, the debtor's bankruptcy petition is something of a restraining order. With it he seeks to prevent an angry creditor from taking legal action which will cut off a portion of his wages and jeopardize his employment.

The deficiency judgment, another collection technique, has been the cause of many a filing. This is a judgment obtained by a creditor following the sale of a piece of property—an automobile or a major appliance, for instance—owned by the debtor. The amount of the judgment is the amount of the balance owed. Often bankrupts feel that deficiency judgments are unjust, that the balance still owed is exorbitant. "He's got the car back. Why should I keep paying him?" they ask.

But, as mentioned above, collection methods, no matter what form they take, must be considered as secondary causes for financial failure, not primary ones. A garnishment is never the reason a critical state of affairs exists; it is the result of it.

Medical debts, money owed doctors and hospitals, are sometimes cited as the reason for a personal bankruptcy. In Dr. Reed's study, no less than 40 percent of the petitioners gave medical indebtedness as a prime reason for their problems. Medical bills do cause travail, but this is usually because the bankrupt-prone individual fails to provide himself with a fund for emergencies. Seldom does he carry a medical insurance plan; he feels that he cannot afford such coverage.

A part of this problem has to do with the low esteem in which medical bills are held by the average person. It is almost traditional that people are less willing to pay a doctor or a dentist than anyone else. These debts accumulate until, in total, they are of significant size.

Of course, sometimes a medical bill can be the cause for genuine financial ruin. In Portland, Oregon, recently a thoroughly solvent, budget-minded couple saw one member of their family struck with cancer—terminal cancer. Nine agonizing months later the patient died. The family, without adequate insurance, found themselves with a $26,000 debt to doctors and hospitals. Bankruptcy was considered as a way out.

Unwise business investments are a contributing factor to the rising bankruptcy rate. It usually happens that the business is put into bankruptcy first, but each partner's involvement is so great, and their losses so severe, that they must later file personal bankruptcy, too. After World War II hundreds of veterans invested their savings in businesses they knew little or nothing about. The records of bankruptcy court during the mid-1940s document their woe. In more recent times the business of bowling serves as an example. It showed spectacular growth during the late 1950s, attracting hundreds of new investors who knew little about the bowling business. But the prosperity wilted in the 1960s. Losses replaced profits, and bowling-center owners by the score sought refuge in bankruptcy proceedings.

There are always cases of people who get into financial stress through no fault of their own. One petitioner wound up in New York's bankruptcy court because his rich uncle left him a farm in Michigan and 500 shares of stock in a New York bank. The county paved the road adjacent to his farm and the assessment was so high he couldn't pay it. The property was sold for taxes. The 500 shares were part of the stock of the Bank of the United States, which failed with a $46 million deficit. Under the law, the New York State Banking Commission ordered him to pay an assessment of $50,000, a sum equal to the value of the stock. In such a situation, bankruptcy was inescapable.

As in any area of business, the bankruptcy field is sprinkled with a few unethical and unscrupulous operators. Sometimes one of these triggers a bankruptcy filing. In California, Ohio and Illinois, states with the highest per-capita rates of bankruptcy, there are cases of unprincipled lawyers who prey on beleaguered debtors. They keep in touch with shop stewards, personnel clerks, loan sharks and pawnbrokers, anyone who can put them in contact with borrowers who are heading for deep trouble. "Don't worry, friend," they tell their clients. "I can get you declared a bankrupt for $50. You won't have to pay anybody, and you can pay me on time." In some areas lawyers place advertisments in the classified sections of the local newspapers to invite prospective clients to take the bankruptcy route. They keep their fees low by dealing in volume, and they have been known to come into court with a batch of ten or fifteen clients, each of whom is paying $75 to $150. In Illinois not too many years ago several lawyers were indicted for promoting a bankruptcy practice for themselves. The New York *Times* reported they had collected $260,000 in fees in ten months.

There are unscrupulous retailers, too. They will advise an account of all the ins and outs of bankruptcy. "It's easy," they say. "Every debt will be wiped out. Just pay me." Dishonesty is also to be found among commercial debt consolidators. They will develop a payment schedule for a debt-ridden client that is wholly unrealistic, extorting fees from the luckless debtor for several months. Then suddenly they announce to him that his case is hopeless, that bankruptcy is the only recourse.

Fortunately, such fraudulence is rare. It is a factor in the growing roster of bankrupts but not a significant one.

Doubtless there are people who enter into bankruptcy proceedings with the idea of evading just debts. But most experts agree that only a small number of petitioners are lacking in moral courage or simply dishonest. To assert that our bankruptcy courts are filled with people intent on fraud does nothing to explain why some states have such a high percapita rate of bankruptcy while in other states the per-capita rate is so low. In Alabama, Arizona, California, Nevada, Oregon and Tennessee there were over 200 bankruptcies per 100,000 population during 1967. In Maryland, North Carolina, Pennsylvania, South Carolina and Texas the per-capita rate was less than ten per 100,000 population for the same year. No one could claim that the people in the first group of states are any less responsible and moral than the citizens of the second group.

The cause of bankruptcy is sometimes a tragic one. Natural disasters—accident, fire, windstorm, flood, theft, any serious loss not covered by insurance—can give rise to a filing. In recent years judgments arising out of automobile accidents have been a cause.

A family that has avoided serious financial difficulty because it has had two pay checks to draw on can easily flounder when its income is halved. This may happen because the wife becomes pregnant or an illness befalls one of the married partners. A change in one's marital status—that is, a separation or a divorce—is a significant factor in some filings.

Max Siporin, in his study "Bankrupt Debtors and Their Families," says that "a spiraling of crises" is what leads to financial downfall. A fire, an accident, a death in the family, a miscarriage, an unplanned pregnancy, the breakdown of the family automobile—a series of critical situations like these often precipitates the larger crisis.

These are the accepted causes of personal bankruptcy in the United States. To sum up, most filings are due to financial mismanagement. In addition, petitioners are victims of easy credit and the insistence on the part of the nation's retailers to buy, buy, buy. Eventually the person's debt becomes so unwieldly that the slightest nudge—an aggressive attempt on the part of the creditor to collect—tumbles him from the precipice.

It should be stressed at this point that bankruptcy is only a small part of the whole problem of credit and collection. It is that part of the iceberg that shows above the water. For every person in bankruptcy court there are at least twenty others experiencing serious difficulty in the handling of their credit obligations. They can be in any one of a number of stages of incipient insolvency. They may be just beginning to fall behind on their payments and have yet to realize the gravity of their situation, or they may have reached that state of indebtedness that renders them vulnerable to the slightest crisis. Bankruptcy is really only a symptom of the greater problem. It is the smoke signal in the distance that keeps telling us that the problem is there.

CHAPTER 10

THE BANKRUPT:
A PROFILE

A great deal is known about the American bankrupt. Indeed, in the past few years he has been pawed and picked over like a piece of discount merchandise on a bargain-basement counter. Eleven studies—most of them prepared by professional researchers and, for the most part, extremely thorough —have tabulated the bankrupt's debts, cataloged his family life and probed his psyche. We have a clear profile of who he is and why he became so laden with debt.

This chapter is based on those studies. The four listed below were considered to be the most revealing.

A prime source in the compilation of these studies was the Statement of Affairs filed by the petitioner, as well as the petition itself. These give information as to the petitioner's assets and liabilities, his occupation, wages, marital status, etc. This information was supplemented through interviews with the petitioners and their attorneys, interviews with referees and court officials, and by information obtained from local credit bureaus and county court records. In each case the researcher received the full cooperation of the local district court.

STUDY AND RESEARCHER	PERIOD COVERED	NUMBER OF CASES
"A Study of Personal Bankruptcy in the Seattle Metropolitan Area," by Dr. John J. Brosky, Assistant Professor of Finance, University of Washington	Sept. '61 to Sept. '64	300
"An Analysis of Economic and Personal Factors Leading to Consumer Bankruptcy (in Flint, Michigan)," by Robert Dolphin, Jr., Assistant Professor, Department of Finance, Florida State University School of Business	Jan. '63 to Dec. '63	486
"Causal Factors in Consumer Bankruptcy (in Northern California): A Case Study," by Robert O. Herrmann, University of California, Davis	Jan. '63 to Dec. '63	74
"Personal Bankruptcies in Oregon," by Edward W. Reed, Professor of Banking and Finance, Bureau of Business and Economic Research, University of Oregon	Jan. '65 to Dec. '65	400

Sex

Most bankrupts are male—indeed, an overwhelming majority of them are. Dolphin's study disclosed that 97 percent of the filings in the Flint, Michigan, area were by males. In other studies males represented as much as 90 percent of the bankrupts. But this should not be taken to mean that bankruptcy is strictly a man's domain, for in his appearance in court he is almost always representing a family unit. Approximately 90 percent of bankrupts are married. Though it is the man who files, women are involved to the degree that it is they who make the family's day-to-day purchases. In the case of major purchases—appliances, automobiles and such—women participate to an important degree.

Some states hold that a wife is liable for the debts of the husband and the family. Thus many of the women who do file petitions do so simply because the husband is filing. Many of the women who do not file coincidentally with a spouse are often separated or divorced. Many have children.

Marital Status

As mentioned above, approximately 90 percent of all bankrupts are married. Yet only about 80 percent of the total male population twenty years old and older is married. This greater incidence of bankruptcy among married persons undoubtedly results from two factors. First, marriage brings additional financial burdens without any increase in the husband's income. Credit is the method the family uses to meet these increased expenses. Second, retailers are somewhat reluctant to grant credit to single men, considering them poor risks. As a result, many single men who are potential bankrupts are screened out.

Bankruptcy-bound couples experience marital difficulties— separation and divorce—to a greater degree than the married population as a whole, although it is a moot point whether the problems of the marriage are caused by financial troubles or vice versa. At any rate, George Allen Brunner, in a study published by Ohio State University which presented tabulations from the court records of 29,332 Ohio bankrupts over a six-year period, found that 17.9 percent of them had experienced marital troubles.

Age

Bankruptcy afflicts the relatively young. The age of those filing covers an extremely wide range, from twenty to sixty-five, but the median age is thirty to thirty-one, or ten to twelve years less than that for male household heads as a whole. In the Dolphin study 72 percent of the bankrupts were under thirty-five. In the Reed study 55 percent were.

Family Size

Though information on this topic is fragmentary, the median number of children in the families of bankrupts has been reported to be three—slightly higher than average. Dolphin found that the mean number of people per bankrupt family to be 4.9, and a rather startling 50 percent of the petitioners had families of five or more. Reed reported the median family size to be 4.3.

Occupation

Every study shows that the so-called "blue collar" worker— that is, the industrial worker, especially the semiskilled or unskilled—is overrepresented among bankrupts. The Brunner study shows this very convincingly. Blue-collar workers constituted an average of 82 percent of the personal bankruptcies over the six-year period covered by the study. Yet, according to the United States Census Bureau, blue-collar workers never accounted for more than 60 percent of the total labor force during the survey period.

Income

Incomes for bankrupts have been found to be slightly below the national average, although Herrmann's study classifies the median income for male bankrupts to be *substantially* lower than the median family income for the country at large. But information on this subject is somewhat deficient. If his wife is employed, the petitioner's Statement of Affairs may not report her income. Exempt income—unemployment compensation or pension income—may go unreported, too.

One reasonable conclusion is possible, however: Bankruptcy is by no means limited to lower-income groups. The median income of the bankrupts in the Reed study was $4,104. Sixty-three percent of the bankrupts in the Dolphin report had incomes of $4,000 a year or more. And a study prepared by Samuel Meyer for Morgan State College in Baltimore (entitled "The Consumer Bankrupt in Maryland") found that the average income of 134 petitioners was $4,752.

Amount and Type of Debt

Each of the studies cited above gives a clear profile of the debts incurred by the petitioner and show that this debt, as to amount and the number of creditors, varies little from region to region. The median of total indebtedness (excluding real-estate mortgages) ranged from $3,661 in the Herrmann study to $4,116 in the Brosky report. Each bankrupt owed approximately fifteen people, although the number ranged from just two to as many as 75.

In character, the debts covered just as wide a range. One petitioner listed $1.25 he owed a newspaper delivery boy.

In each study, however, a major portion of the petitioner's debt accumulation was represented by money due bankers, loan companies and other lending institutions (exclusive of real-estate mortgages). In the Reed study, more bankrupts— 64 percent—owed secured debts to consumer finance companies than to any other creditor. Consumer finance debt was also the largest in amount. Debts to financial institutions represented 47 percent of the total indebtedness in the Dolphin study. The Brosky report disclosed that petitioners owed a median of $1,258 to small-loan and sales-finance companies. In each case a majority of the petitioners listed two or more small-loan and sales-finance companies.

The second most important category of debt was represented by money due retailers for small merchandise items. In the Herrmann study, 89 percent of the petitioners listed debts of this type, though the amounts were not large, averaging a total of about $190. In the Brosky report, too, the petitioners were found to be heavily involved with retail credit grantors, such as automobile dealers and garages, department stores, clothing stores, fuel-oil dealers, lumber yards, delicatessens and dairies.

Money owed for medical and dental services is a third important category, and often this is of a significant amount. In the Brosky study, 269 petitioners listed medical bills; the median amount owed was $387.50. A total of 108 of these owed medical bills in excess of $500. Eighty-five percent of the bankrupts in the Reed study owed some medical debt. The median was $184. One petitioner owed 24 medical bills. When confronted with this statistic, one doctor shrugged. "You have to expect it," he said. "After all, you can't repossess an appendix."

Bankrupts also listed a variety of other debts which can only be termed "miscellaneous." They owed landlords and utility companies, jewelry stores and pharmacies, hobby shops and reducing salons, insurance agents and veterinarians. Any individual or business which sold goods or performed services on credit was fair game.

What kind of person goes bankrupt? The answer is clear. He is between thirty and thirty-five, married and with a larger than average family. He is a blue-collar worker, with an annual income of about $4,500. At the time of his filing he owes about fifteen people about $4,000, not including his mortgage, if he has a home.

For more than a year the pressure has been steadily building, and now his debt load is of unmanageable proportions. His mailbox is stuffed with angry letters. He no longer answers his telephone. He even dodges friends on the street. The chances are one in five that at least one creditor has begun some form of legal action.

His relative youth, his lack of financial experience, the burden of his large family—all these play a part. Bankruptcy offers "immediate" relief. But he really knows no other course. One morning he stands solemnly before the referee in federal district court and becomes a bankruptcy statistic. Any feeling of shame or guilt is dissipated by the sense of relief he gets in knowing that he is free from threats of garnishment and other forms of debtor harassment.

Many bankrupts pledge that they will pay back the money they owe, even though they have obtained a discharge. But few ever do. One study has reported that less than one-half of 1 percent of the money owed is repaid. It is much more likely that the petitioner will resume his credit spending and be in debt again—perhaps heavily—within a year. And the chances are one in fifteen that six years hence will be back in bankruptcy court.

CHAPTER 11

BANKRUPTCY
AND THE POOR

The first Bankruptcy Act was written for the rich, for the monied merchant class of the country, and even until fairly recent times the filing of a petition was regarded as a privilege of the fairly well-to-do in our society. No more. Consumer-education experts representing the low-income neighborhoods of big cities look on bankruptcy as one way of righting the wrongs perpetrated by unscrupulous merchants who feed on the poor. More and more this course is being recommended to those who have been victimized.

"We're telling people who have a lot of debts to file bankruptcy," says Mrs. Florence Rice, head of the Harlem Consumer Education Council in New York City. "People who are on the verge of going on welfare because of debt, anyone who finds himself deep in debt and can't pay off—we're advising these people to wipe the slate clean and go bankrupt."

"If enough people do it on a big scale we may be able to get some changes on the terrible credit swindling that goes on among the poor."

Julius Hobson, head of ACT, a militant civil-rights organization, has drawn plans to urge poor Negroes across the country to go bankrupt. Says Mr. Hobson: "Can you imagine what it will mean to poor black people, most of whom are victims of unconscionable contracts and usurious interest rates?"

It is a matter of regrettable fact that fraud is rife in the ghetto neighborhoods of the big cities of the United States. The poor are easy prey. Unable to obtain credit from conventional sources and unsophisticated in their buying habits, they stand ready to be duped. They are victims of exorbitant credit and carrying charges, undue sales pressure, deceptive pricing and false advertising.

Sometimes the fraud is a simple one and involves just a small amount of money. When Mrs. Smith moved into a city-financed housing project on New York City's lower East Side, she and her family had the first bathroom that they didn't have to share with anyone else. They also had their first shower. The movers had hardly left when a door-to-door salesman appeared and offered Mrs. Smith a selection of brightly colored shower curtains. "Not today," she said. But the salesman persisted, explaining how she could get the curtains for "only" a dollar a week for twelve weeks. Mrs. Smith went along. A few days later she saw in Macy's the same type of shower curtain as the one she had chosen. It was priced at three dollars.

Often, however, the schemes are more devious and the amount of money involved is significant. Unscrupulous furniture dealers operate a typical racket. A store will take a full page in a daily newspaper to advertise "three rooms of furniture for $117." When the buyer goes to the store, he is told the furniture is "gone," but then the salesman tries to sell him something for $800 or $900 on an installment plan.

If he signs up, he's in trouble. Not long after the merchandise is delivered defects begin to appear. Fabrics start to shred at the seams. Heat dries out the glue that held the furniture together; table and chairs fall apart. Often when the customer returns to the store to complain he is told that his installment contract has been sold to a credit company and the store is no longer responsible for the goods purchased.

The finance company that has purchased the installment contract will not listen to his complaints. It wants its money— every month. If the customer lags in payment, the finance company has the right to force payment, perhaps by garnishing the debtor's salary. Or he may repossess the merchandise and then press for payment on the balance due.

Such practices aren't limited to just furniture by any means. "Here's a sewing machine for just fifteen dollars," a door-to-door salesman tells the unwary housewife. The machine, of course, is worthless. All the salesman wants to do is talk her into buying a $250 machine on an installment plan. Expensive books and encyclopedias are also sold door to door, with the salesman using a "Don't-you-want-to-help-your-child?" pitch.

Consumers so victimized are prime candidates for bankruptcy. When they realize that they have been cheated they feel little obligation to pay.

Another method of swindle involves revolving credit contracts. Under the terms of such contracts a customer can utilize his original installment agreement to make additional purchases. But here's the catch: If a person defaults on a payment the retailer can repossess any or all of the purchases. A Bronx truck driver was injured on his job and forced to take a leave of absence. He fell behind in his payments to a neighborhood furniture–appliance store when he owed about $150 on a color television set. The store repossessed not only the set but also dining-room furniture and a washer-dryer combination, other items that he had charged to the revolving account.

A highly regarded and much quoted survey by David Caplovitz of Columbia University's Bureau of Applied Re-

search is entitled "The Poor Pay More." Caplovitz studied
464 low-income families living in public-housing projects in
New York City and concluded that the poor are the unwitting
purchasers of costly merchandise. The families he interviewed
spent a high percentage of their incomes on major appliances
and for furnishing their homes and apartments. Invariably they
bought on credit and at perilously high rates of interest.

Part of the problem is a lack of education and sophistication.
"The ghetto poor are easily deceived," says Mrs. Rice. "They
confuse quantity and quality when they're shopping. They
thing that because they're getting four rooms of furniture for
$495 that they're getting a great buy. They don't stop to
realize what kind of furniture it is."

While there are exceptions, the intelligent and prudent use
of money is regarded by many specialists to be most lacking
in those families classed as "poor"—those with annual incomes
of less than $3,000. Dr. Louise C. Richards, now a research
psychologist with the Consumer Survey Branch of the U.S.
Food and Drug Administration, found that among the poor
who buy durable goods (an automobile, a major appliance or
furniture) in a given year, the purchase accounts for a "start-
lingly high" proportion of their income. Among those families
who bought a "major durable" and whose annual income was
less than $2,000, an average of 48 percent of that income went
toward installment payments. Among those whose income was
$2,000 to $4,999, the share was 28 percent. (More than 15
percent is considered imprudent.)

These families seldom exhibited economical practices, said
Dr. Richards. They were less deliberate when shopping than
upper-income families. They were less price conscious. They
did not search out good buys. They were less informed about
the quality characteristics of the products they bought.

"Many factors converge in making installment debt an

especially pressing problem for the poor," says Dr. Richards. Besides not knowing how to shop, they encounter credit costs higher than average. And because they usually deal with small merchants and neighborhoods stores, they are charged higher prices.

Caplovitz has called attention to a ghetto phenomenon he calls "compensatory consumption," where a person with little or no status tends to fill the vacuum with goods. This is one way of explaining why $8 million worth of Cadillacs were brought into New York City's Harlem in 1965. In our society, self-respect and the respect accorded others is often based on material possessions, a fact that presents the low-income consumer with an agonizing dilemma.

There are no simple solutions to the problems confronting the ghetto poor. Caplovitz believes that cooperative stores would help. Credit unions have been suggested.

Twenty-three states have Consumer Fraud Bureaus patterned after the one set up in New York State by Attorney General Louis Lefkowitz. But their failing is that the Attorney General has no power to prosecute the perpetrators of fraud.

"If consumer fraud is to be done away with, it is essential that there be strong enforcement machinery and that the perpetrators of such fraud be confronted with criminal sanctions," Caplovitz told a House of Representatives subcommittee recently. "Until strong enforcement machinery is instituted, I see little hope of making much headway in eliminating fraud."

The Office of Economic Opportunity is helping to assuage the credit-debt problems of poverty-stricken families. Through 1966 the agency had made 56 grants totaling almost $3 million to support consumer education and related programs. These programs concentrated on providing legal services and financial counseling.

Bankruptcy is regarded as one short-term solution to financial problems of the poor. OEO legal counselors have no hesitancy in recommending it when it is deemed the best course of action for a particular individual.

"No one in Harlem ever considered going bankrupt a few years ago," states Mrs. Rice. "They thought it was only something a businessman could do. They'd see a storeowner go out of business in one location and a couple of weeks later set up shop in another. Well, they're beginning to get the idea. In another year or two things are going to be different."

CHAPTER **12**

THE CREDIT
BOOM

"Consumer credit has become an essential feature of the American way of life. It permits families with secure and growing incomes to plan ahead and to enjoy fully and promptly the ownership of automobiles and modern household appliances. It finances higher education for many who otherwise could not afford it. To families struck by serious illness or other financial setbacks, the opportunity to borrow eases the burden by spreading the payments over time."

These words were spoken not by the head of the National Foundation for Consumer Credit but by the President of the United States in a message to Congress on February 16, 1967. The only thing wrong with the President's statement is that it did not go far enough. Credit today is much more than just "an essential feature" of the American way of life; to some it *is* the American way of life.

Consumer credit has wrought its influence on the American economy for only the last fifty years or so. The practice of using credit to finance the purchase of automobiles and other expensive durable goods began in the days just before World War I and developed rapidly during the 1920s. Credit today, of course, is used to purchase not only expensive durable goods but also non-durable goods and an ever-growing number of services, including the lending of money. The use of credit is now so widespread in the United States that it is extremely unusual for the individual or family not to owe somebody something.

"Consumer credit," to the Federal Reserve System, "includes all short- and intermediate-term credit that is extended through regular business channels to finance the purchase of commodities and services for personal consumption, or to refinance debts incurred for such purposes." It may be either one of two types: non-installment or installment. Non-installment consumer credit, or single-payment credit, is the kind used in paying utility bills, thirty-day open charge accounts, credit-card accounts and the dentist or the doctor.

Installment credit is the kind that requires two or more payments. There are four types. First, there is automobile "paper"—that is, promissory notes extended for the purchase of new cars. Second, installment credit includes the credit granted for any non-automotive consumer goods—appliances, furniture, jewelry, boats or mobile homes. These two types of credit may be extended directly from the retailer to the consumer, but in many cases the credit grantor will sell the paper, accepting cash for it from a sales finance company, a commercial bank or some other lending institution. The consumer then owes the sales finance company, not the original credit grantor.

A third type of installment credit is that represented by repair and modernization loans made to consumers by the Federal Housing Administration enabling them to finance the maintenance or improvement of their homes. Such credit is also used for the purchase and installation of heating and air-conditioning equipment, storm windows and kitchen equipment, as well as for major additions or alterations.

Last, installment credit takes the form of installment loans—

that is, any type of loan not covered in the other three categories. Loans are obtained for any number of reasons— to pay medical expenses, for travel or educational expenses or for the payment of taxes or insurance premiums.

Through the use of consumer credit, people are able to buy and enjoy goods that they otherwise could not afford. Or they are able to finance purchases without disturbing their savings or investments. Not only has consumer credit thus been of value to the purchaser but, by supplementing existing purchasing power, it has also tended to stimulate production and employment. It has wrought an enormously beneficial effect on the country as a whole.

Statistics concerning consumer credit indicate that the current boom may have gone about as far as it can go. The number of personal bankruptcies is at a record level. And about 120,000 Americans lost their homes in 1967 through mortgage foreclosures. There is other evidence.

In March 1967 the Board of Governors of the Federal Reserve System reported that the American consumer owed an astonishing $92.5 billion to department stores and discount houses, to banks and finance companies, a figure that averaged out to about $500 in indebtedness for every man, woman and child in the country, and this was a figure that did not include home mortgages. This is 2.2 times the total in 1957.

The most significant development in consumer credit has been the rapid growth of installment credit. Of the $92.5 billion, $73.5 billion was of the installment type. The largest chunk of this was $30.5 billion in automobile paper. Personal loans accounted for another $20 billion of the total.

Adding in the mortgage debt, which totaled approximately $220 billion in March 1967, the grand total came to $312 billion, or only $18 billion less than the total national debt of the United States government.

Fully one half of all American families are now paying one type or another of installment debt. And one half of these are our poorest citizens, families with incomes of $3,000 a year or less. These families are spending at least 20 percent of their incomes to pay what they owe.

When mortgage money is included, Commerce Department figures show that the average American family is using about one quarter of its take-home income to repay installment loans and mortgages and their attendant finance charges. To put it in another way, the average family now works three months a year simply to pay off its debts.

As a result of the nation's credit-buying binge, credit has become much more than just a selling tool for the retailer. It has become a business in itself. Consider this statistic: In 1966 consumers paid approximately $11 billion in finance charges on their short- and intermediate-term indebtedness of $92.5 billion. By contrast, the federal government paid only $11 billion in interest on its national debt of $330 billion. So not only is credit a business in itself; it is a *big* business. Many hard-goods retailers are now in the banking business. Their net profit does not depend so much on what the consumer pays over and above the wholesale price of the merchandise; instead it hinges on the amount of the carrying charges—that is, the interest paid by the customer.

Some of the nation's largest retailers now derive an important part of their income from credit charges. Sears, Roebuck, Montgomery Ward, W. T. Grant, J. C. Penney, Alden's and Gamble-Skogmo are not merely merchandisers; they also conduct vast finance-company operations resulting from the enormous amount of credit purchases consumers make.

Quite logically, the reverse is also taking place—major loan companies are buying control of merchandising chains. Household Finance Company now owns the White Stores, Coast-to-

Coast Stores and Ben Franklin Stores. Beneficial Finance Company owns Spiegel's and also Western Auto Supply. These retail outlets produce credit accounts for the finance company end of the business.

The nation's credit grantors have developed a studied complacency toward the country's credit boom. Any proposal to tighten credit is loudly opposed because of the deleterious effect it might have on the economy. Instead, efforts are made to keep the boom going.

Bank credit cards are a case in point. A recent innovation, bank credit cards are similar to the cards issued by the American Express Company and the Diners' Club, but they are not meant so much for business executives who seek to document expense-account entertainment; they are more for middle-income families and their day-to-day needs and pleasures. Not only are bank cards good for the purchase of retail merchandise, but in some cities doctors and dentists accept them. In Chicago several mortuaries signed up.

Bank cards have the added feature of permitting the holders to charge small loans. In the past, banks found that it was poor economics to handle loans of $100 or less for sixty to ninety days; it cost them more to process the account than the law would allow them to charge. But with credit cards they can service this type of account with profit.

Most bank cards cost consumers nothing—so long as they pay their bills at the bank within thirty days. If they don't, the bank assesses the account what has been called "a small monthly charge" but what is in reality a highly profitable 1½ percent rate of interest.

In the year prior to April 1967 more than one thousand banks began promoting their own credit-card systems. The methods of promotion raised eyebrows. A number of banks in the Midwest, operating together, "mailed out mounds of credit cards unsolicited to each other's customers and former customers," *The Wall Street Journal* recently reported. An official of Chase Manhattan Bank in New York City explained this policy. "To choke off competition, you must flood the market with cards. Everybody gets cards from every bank he does or does not do business with. People who may have a capacity to repay $500 may have received cards from various banks that could permit them to charge up to $3,000 or $4,000!"

Bank credit cards have bruised the nation's credit system in at least one other way. Many of these cards can be used to charge mail or telephone orders; thus a card can be used by some person other than the one to whom it was issued. In 1966, when Chicago banks initiated their card plans, they were hit by widespread thefts of cards by postal employees that resulted in severe losses.

Banks have been less than judicious in checking the credit of their prospective cardholders, a failing that has earned them the criticism of Betty Furness, President Johnson's Special Assistant for Consumer Affairs. She quotes a survey of the Consumer Bankers Association which declares that almost one half of the banks five million new card offerings were made without credit checks. New York City's First National City Bank was responsible for putting one of its "Everything" cards into the hands of a customer against whom they held a $1,500 judgment for defaulting on a personal loan. "Can I use the card to satisfy the judgment?" he wanted to know.

Using credit today is incredibly simple. But in the future it promises to be easier still. Financial experts representing the American Bankers Association believe that a nationwide system of automated transfers of money and credit, completely eliminating the need for cash or even checks, is possible within the next fifteen years.

A pilot project of this type is already in operation at the Bank of Delaware in Wilmington. It works like this: A clerk in a store that is tied in to the bank's equipment inserts the plastic identification card of the credit customer into a slot in a touch-tone card-dialer telephone, presses a few buttons to indicate the amount of the purchase, and completes a charge or cash transaction through the Bank of Delaware without involving a single piece of paper. The whole operation takes just seconds. New York's Irving Trust Company and Detroit's Manufacturers National have ordered similar equipment to register cash transfers among businessmen.

No one has analyzed how a cashless, checkless, computerized credit system will affect the unsophisticated and impulsive buyer and borrower, nor has anyone reasoned how he is going to affect it. And what will such a system do to the rising rate of bankruptcies? No one knows that either.

CHAPTER 13

CREDIT:
USE AND ABUSE

While credit is a boon to the average consumer, enabling him to enjoy goods and services that he might otherwise have to do without, it is very much of a two-edged sword. Its use can be advantageous; it can also be deadly.

A Los Angeles referee in bankruptcy states that most of the people that come before him are "lost" in the economic system that prevails. "They are enticed, urged and badgered to buy things that they don't need and can't afford," he says.

A referee in Denver says that most bankrupts show little resistance to the "hard sell," whether it is personal or by mail. By noting how frequently the names of companies appear on the listings of creditors filed by bankruptcy petitioners, the referee said that he could tell which local retailers and mail-order houses have put on aggressive campaigns for installment buyers.

These examples suggest a problem that has two parts. It is a case of retailers overselling or deliberately misleading and consumers who have little knowledge of how to buy or desire to budget.

Too many prospective debtors never really acquire an understanding of what credit costs. And it does cost. Credit is a service, and those who use it must pay service charges. These include the interest or "rent" on the credit grantor's money, the cost of processing the repayments, the cost of the credit investigation and the amount that the credit grantor had to pay for the funds in the first place—many, many different factors. In the end, the finance charge is established by considering almost as many multiples as the Ford Company ponders in pricing a new automobile.

Confusion in the minds of consumers about the cost of credit sometimes exists because they are faced with a bewildering array of carrying charges and compound interest rates. In the case of simple loans—that is, where the principal is paid back in its entirety at the end of the loan period—the rate of interest is not hard to figure. The grade-school formula applies: Interest equals principal times the rate times the time. In the case of a loan of $1,000 for a year at 6 percent, the borrower must pay interest of $60. But finance charges are seldom if ever that easy to compute.

For instance, often the consumer, when dealing with a bank, becomes involved in the use of an installment repayment plan. This is usually arranged on a monthly basis over the term of the loan. This complicates the figuring of the actual rate of interest. Suppose a person borrows $1,000 for a year at an interest rate of $60 and repays the loan in twelve equal monthly installments. The actual rate of interest here is not 6 percent but almost 12 percent (provided the borrower received the full $1,000 and not a "discounted" loan of $940). The interest rate spirals to 12 percent because the customer has the use of only one half of the actual amount borrowed, on the average, over the course of the year.

This is only one way in which the cost of credit is made obscure. There are at least five others.

Sometimes the rate of interest is not given to the consumer. He is told he will pay so much down and so much a month. Neither the rate of interest nor the total finance charge is disclosed. In some cases even the total number of payments is left untold. The customer continues to pay until he realizes that he is the victim of a fraud.

A second and frequent method is to express the finance charge in "dollars per $100," with the debt to be repaid in equal monthly installments. For example, a borrower may be told he is being granted a "6 percent loan." But since he is paying in installments, the actual rate of interest is almost double, or 12 percent. This rate is further inflated by an "add in" gimmick. The borrower receives $100 in cash but has to pay back $106, the principal plus the reputed rate of interest.

A third method of concealing the true cost of credit is by discounting the amount borrowed. Many banks do this. The person who borrows $100 receives only $94, but he must pay back the full amount. Again the interest is expressed as "6 percent." And again the actual rate is slightly more than 12 percent.

A fourth method is to express a loan's interest by means of a monthly rate. The customer may be told that the finance rate is 2 percent a month. The annual rate is 12 times two, or 24 percent, if the interest is based on the unpaid balance. Most consumer finance companies operate in this fashion.

A few credit grantors charge interest "per month on the original balance." Such a moneylender may advertise his rate as "2 percent a month," but the 2 percent, when applied to the original balance throughout the term of the loan, builds to a formidable level. A borrower accepting $100 at this rate is making interest payments of $24—$2 a month. But the hitch is this: Since he pays back the loan in equal monthly installments, the average amount he owes over the entire year is

$50. And a $24 annual interest charge for the use of $50 is a simple interest rate of 48 percent!

In a fifth method the lender seeks to confuse the customer by loading on all sorts of extra charges. While the interest rate may appear low, the borrower is also asked to pay for such as credit investigation, processing fees, credit life insurance and a finders fee. In total it adds up to a bad deal.

Commercial banks are the largest single source of consumer credit. There are more than 13,000 of them throughout the country. Credit unions and consumer finance companies are also important. A word about the latter. In the early 1900s banks were much more reluctant to lend money than they are today. People who are refused loans by banks had to turn to loan sharks for money. As an alternative, and to force usurious lenders out of business, small-loan companies were encouraged. Since they lent only small amounts of money, they were given the right to charge higher-than-bank rates of interest. Today there are about 2,000 consumer finance companies, all closely regulated by state laws. They operate more than 13,000 offices.

Small-loan companies are often accused of adding to a person's financial stress by virtue of the high interest rates they charge. But when the amount borrowed is small, the finance charge is really not significant. For instance, a $100 loan at the annual rate of 36 percent can be paid off in twelve installments of $10.05 each. The price of borrowing the $100 is $20.60, not exorbitant for someone who needs $100.

What the less scrupulous finance companies do is attempt to "boost" loans. A person who seeks $100 for three months is likely to wind up with twice that amount and with payments spread out over a year. "You're getting $200 and the payments are less," the sales pitch goes. Another play is to renew the loan. A customer who is delinquent a payment or two may be asked to refinance the total amount due. "It'll make your payments a lot smaller, a lot easier," he's told. The debtor ends up paying interest charges on top of interest charges—a dangerous procedure.

The bankruptcy petition of a Des Moines man, his debts nearly twice his assets, shows the lack of wisdom in taking one loan to pay another. Among his unsecured debts were five loans from five small-loan companies. The first loan was for only $16, but each one of the others was progressively larger. The last loan was $2,044.32. He had gotten into debt; then, unable to pay, he had taken out a loan. Unable to pay that, he had taken out another, and so on. "People think they can borrow themselves out of debt," said the referee. "But they just can't."

It is not only the unsophisticated borrower who is bewildered. When testifying before the Senate Banking Subcommittee, one witness stated, "It has been confusing to me, on a number of occasions on transactions that I have been involved in, to try to figure out just what it [credit cost] really is. . . . Not only are the present practices confusing, but how you figure is confusing." The witness was William McChesney Martin, Chairman of the Board of Governors of the Federal Reserve System.

In an effort to put a measure of restraint on those who abuse the credit system, Congress passed a "Truth in Lending" bill in May 1968. It would require merchants, retailers and lending institutions to inform their customers of the annual rate of interest that they will be paying and also the total amount of the finance charges. Senator Paul Douglas of Illinois first introduced such legislation in 1960, but opposition to the bill—from finance companies, automobile dealers and state and national retail organizations—was widespread and intense. Senator Douglas' bill and other and similar bills introduced in ensuing years were successfully bottled up in committee. When, in 1967, the Truth-in-Lending measure first reached the floor of the Senate, it passed unanimously, 92–0.

This bill, however, contained a major compromise in that it exempted stores and banks that offer revolving credit from stating the annual interest rate. They were required to give customers only the monthly rate of interest, what stores call a "service charge."

Common to all department stores and many large retailers, revolving credit accounts permit a customer to charge new purchases, even if he has not completely paid for previous ones, as long as he makes regular monthly payments on the outstanding balance. Revolving accounts used to be geared to the purchase of soft household goods and clothing, and each account had a set limit on the amount that could be charged. Usually this was from $50 to $250, and the customer agreed to pay for all purchases within a specified period, usually four months.

But revolving credit accounts have outgrown these restraints. Today, large appliances—a refrigerator, for instance—can often be purchased by means of revolving credit. The customer is saved the bother of signing an installment contract. The agreement that he entered into at the time he opened his account serves. Instead of being limited to four payments, he is allowed ten or twelve. Revolving credit accounts go by an assortment of names. Sometimes they are called All Purpose Accounts. When applied to long-term transactions, they may be known as Continuous Secured Accounts.

In theory, a revolving credit works like this: On an automatic washer which costs $188 there is no service charge for the first thirty days, provided a payment of one tenth or one twelfth of the cost is made the first month. Beginning with the second month, an average charge of 1½ percent is levied on the unpaid balance. The charge is continued on the unpaid balance while monthly payments reduce it or new purchases are made which increase it.

But between theory and practice there is a wide gap, and a customer who attempts to ascertain what interest charges he is paying on his revolving credit account is likely to find himself painfully bewildered. The puzzle is trying to establish how much of the balance due is subject to the service charge. The muddle that can be created is best evidenced by these excerpts from the contract applications of three mail-order houses:

Sears, Roebuck & Co.: ". . . an amount of time price differential computed at 1½% of balance at the beginning of each monthly billing period until the full amount of all purchases and time price differential thereon are paid in full."

Montgomery Ward & Co.: ". . . a time price differential or service charge of 1½% per month on the opening monthly balance of any account on amounts up to $500 and 1% per month on amounts in excess of $500."

J. C. Penney Co.: ". . . a time price differential ('service charge') computed by applying the rate of 1½% to the unpaid balance of the cash sale price and any unpaid service charge on each of any monthly billing dates (pursuant to your then current billing schedule) commencing with the second monthly billing date following the date of purchase . . ."

Professor Richard L. D. Morse of Kansas State University has studied the tangle of revolving credit in depth. Comparing six different systems of well-known merchandisers, he showed how interest charges can run twice as high in some stores as in others.

Merchants and bankers argue that revolving credit should be exempt from the provisions of the Truth-in-Lending measure because the service charge is different for each person. While the interest rate is (usually) 1½ percent a month for everyone, this does not always translate into 18 percent. It is usually lower, retailers claim, because a customer who buys something shortly after his monthly bills have been made out could have as long as 59 days of interest-free time. (However, if the customer fails to pay in full on or before the ninth day, he is charged interest from the date of the purchase.) Notwithstanding the arguments put forth by retailers and banks, there are a number of simple yardsticks that could be applied for pricing revolving credit at competing banks and stores. Standardizing the billing systems is just one of them.

Former Senator Douglas, testifying before a subcommittee of the House of Representatives, declared that some experts had predicted that one half of all consumer credit would be revolving credit within five years. The fact that the Senate granted an exemption to revolving credit in its Truth-in-Lending measure "could grow into an enormous loophole," Mr. Douglas said. It is more than just a loophole; it is a yawning escape route for the retailer and banker.

After the Senate's passage of the bill, Mrs. Leonor K. Sullivan, a member of the House of Representatives from St. Louis, introduced a Truth-in-Lending measure in the House. Known as the "Consumer Credit Protection Act," this was regarded as a "tougher" bill than the Senate measure, and it restored the provision requiring retailers to inform their customers of the annual rate of interest they pay on revolving charge accounts. This provision was included in the Truth-in-Lending bill that Congress passed in May 1968. It was also made to apply to loans and installment purchases in general. In other words, finance companies, banks, other lenders, and retailers must inform borrowers and credit customers of credit charges in terms of annual percentage rates.

A Truth-in-Lending law went into effect in Massachusetts in January 1967, the first state law of its type to be passed.

It required lenders to explain in detail the costs of a loan, spelling out in detail the interest rate on an annual basis. This information has to be printed on the loan contract in large type. If a creditor fails to disclose the required information, he can be prevented from claiming any of the normal finance and collection charges.

The federal government's Truth-in-Lending measure, and state laws such as the one in Massachusetts, are a move in the right direction. By requiring full disclosure of credit charges, they better enable the consumer to make a direct comparison of the cost of credit. Thus he can shop for the best "buy." Proponents of these measures say that they may even stimulate price competition within the credit industry.

While Truth-in-Lending legislation can be a blessing for the average consumer, it is not a cure to the credit ills that exist. Not by any means. Such legislation does almost nothing to protect the consumer from the unscrupulous retailer or money-lender. And it does not protect the consumer from himself. True, the credit use can be hopelessly confused by the array of "add ons," "discounts," "service charges" and "finance charges" that can be associated with installment purchases or loans. These can make it almost impossible for all but the most mathematically astute individuals to compute the real cost of a credit purchase. But it is often the case that a prospective buyer will not even bother to consider the rate of interest he is being asked to pay, and even the total cost is not altogether important to him. Instead, he asks, "How much is the down payment? How much is the monthly payment?"

The management official of a New England supermarket chain tells this story. One morning he was startled to see a stock clerk at one of his stores drive to work in a late-model Cadillac. The executive asked the young man to explain. "A Cadillac doesn't cost any more than a Chevrolet," the clerk said. "You just pay a little longer." This is not an isolated instance. In 1961 three out of every five new-car loans were written with payment plans that stretched for thirty months or more. But in 1965 four out of every five auto loans were written that way.

Most bankruptcy-prone individuals are unrealistic in the purchases they make. Their debts often are far more long-lasting than what they buy. Automobiles are a common example of this. Many petitioners list loans for cars they no longer own.

Carelessness in credit buying is also characterized by a failure to realize the hidden expenses that some purchases lead to. A color television set, financed over a two-year period, may be well within a family's budget. But in addition to the cost of the set and the interest payments, the family may have to bear delivery charges, the purchase price and installation charge for an antenna, and repair and service fees for as long as they have the set. These additional expenses may put the set out of financial reach. An automobile is another item wherein charges for operation and upkeep are as much of a burden as the original cost.

One of the most informative recent studies of the overextended credit family was one conducted by Dr. Milton J. Huber, associate professor of the Center for Consumer Affairs of the University of Wisconsin. The survey focused on the buying habits of 100 Detroit families, all of whom were overburdened with debt. The project was financed by a grant from the MacGregor Fund of Michigan and staffed by students and researchers from the Merrill-Palmer Institute of Human Development and Family Life, the Michigan Credit Union League, the Wayne State University School of Social Work, and the Center for Consumer Affairs of the University of Wisconsin Extension Division.

The study revealed that the great majority of the families interviewed possessed two dominant personal characteristics: They were impulsive; they had a complacent, even a carefree attitude. When impulsiveness applies to credit buying and complacency to debt, financial calamity can be the only result.

In their installment purchases these families were found to prefer "easy credit" merchants whenever they were buying furniture or household appliances. On the average, 54.3 percent of each family's income was committed to such purchases.

They shopped at discount houses and supermarkets for their clothing and food. Most of the families admitted that they could not resist the persuasiveness of door-to-door salesmen. Several stated that they finally refused to answer the door when a salesman rang. They knew they were too weak. Dr. Huber said the families showed "limited pleasure postponing mechanism."

The families listed driving, picnicking and camping as major outdoor diversions. The husbands enjoyed softball and bowling. To every member of the family, television was an important form of recreation. Few of the men and women interviewed did much reading. Even newspapers were not read.

The families averaged eleven years of marriage and had three children. Most declared that their financial problems began during the early years of marriage. Almost 30 percent disclosed that trouble with money began with the marriage, and 10 percent said they were experiencing such problems during their courtship.

The average annual income for the families was $6,504, against an indebtedness of $3,689. But 50 percent of the families reported declining incomes, and in one third of these the drop was drastic. Another third reported rising incomes. Thus virtually all of the families were experiencing a fluctuation in earnings and were being subjected to the accompanying stresses and adjustments.

Dr. Huber stated that there was a "confusion of roles" between the married partners. Almost one half of them demonstrated a lack of cooperative decision-making or intelligent planning. One husband expressed it this way: "We don't argue over it. If either of us wants something, we buy it."

CHAPTER 14

CREDIT LOOPHOLES

It's ironic, but the people most seriously injured by bankruptcy proceedings—retail credit grantors—have at their disposal one of the most effective methods of controlling credit losses. This is credit information as provided by a local board of trade, a merchants' association, a lenders' exchange, and particularly by a local credit bureau.

A credit bureau is a storehouse of facts concerning consumers in a given trading area. Its major purpose is to gather and report all types of information regarding a person's buying and paying habits. It makes this information available to business and professional people for their confidential use in extending credit.

Credit bureaus are about as widespread as department stores. Almost all of them are members of the Associated Credit Bureaus of America, Inc., which has its headquarters in Houston, Texas. Associated Credit Bureaus has more than 4,200 members serving 360,000 credit grantors in 36,000 communities throughout the United States, Canada and several foreign countries.

The files of a credit bureau contain information from the ledgers of all types of credit grantors and from public records on marriages, divorces, births and deaths. Courthouse records are checked for chattel mortgages, liens, bankruptcy filings, deeds, etc. Police records are noted, and sometimes newspaper items containing vital facts are clipped and placed in the record.

A credit file usually contains the following types of information:

* Identification: name of the head of the household, his full address, his Social Security number, name of his spouse, her Social Security number.

* Present employment: name of his employer and his kind of business, position, length of time in present position, monthly income.

* Personal history: date of birth, number of dependents, homeowner or not, former address, former employment, spouse's employment.

* Public record: court record, chattel mortgages, suits or judgments if any, changes in marital status, etc.

* Credit history: previous and current credit accounts showing date each account opened, highest credit, amount owing if any, amount past due if any, kind of account—open, revolving or installment—and usual manner of payment.

To secure information from a credit bureau a firm must be a "member." Membership is usually on a contractual basis, but it is normally open to all credit grantors in a community. It is refused to any firm whose operations are construed to be of an illegal nature or demonstrably harmful to the public good. A membership contract normally requires that the member will provide credit information to the bureau on request.

Credit reports can be obtained over the telephone or by means of a standard report form. Through a local bureau a credit grantor can obtain a report from any city in the United States within a few days. Thus a local merchant can determine whether a new resident is a person to be considered a good risk.

When a retailer does obtain information from a credit bureau he has to interpret it properly. For instance, he may get a favorable report on a person, but if the customer's current pay check seems scarcely able to support his charge-account activity, the retailer should put a limit on the amount of credit he allows the new account.

Sometimes a retailer can perceive trouble ahead by a customer's behavior when he is opening an account. Anyone who appears anxious to buy great quantities of merchandise the moment he is handed his credit card is a potential source of trouble. Another is the customer who flourishes an excessive number of identifying credentials when making his credit application.

The fact that a customer has a dozen charge accounts but not the kind of income to support them should be another caution signal to the retailer. Warning could also come in the form of a credit check that reveals a prospective customer has just opened charge accounts in several stores at the same time. He might be planning to embark on a wild buying spree, a trait common to more than a few bankrupts in the months just before they file.

Of course, sometimes even the most painstaking credit investigation does not reveal that an account is going to be troublesome. In some cases the customer simply doesn't pay.

The country's credit-reporting system is not perfect by any means. It has a number of failings that work to the aid of the individual who is seemingly intent on achieving bankruptcy. For instance—and this is not uncommon at all—a buyer or borrower in making an application for credit is likely to list only those references that he feels will give him a favorable report. And since sellers and lenders generally query only those references given by the prospective debtor, they learn nothing adverse about him.

There are other shortcomings. Sometimes credit grantors are remiss in reporting information about their accounts, failing to notify the local bureau when an account becomes past due or is placed for collection. The result is that people who are in debt are permitted to become more heavily burdened.

In addition, no one credit bureau possesses all the information about an individual. Local bureaus compete, almost as any other type of business. Some do not research or file court findings. An individual credit grantor may furnish information to only one bureau and ignore the others. The result is that local retailers are sometimes not given the whole story about a prospective purchaser. A way to overcome this problem is to establish one central credit file for each city or trading area. As business and credit information become more computerized, this may become possible.

These deficiences are not altogether serious. What is much worse is the fact that a growing number of retailers and moneylenders turn a deaf ear to credit reports. Their excuse is that the pressure of competition forces them to be negligent. In other words, "Get the business!" is the battle cry.

The results of a recent study of 1,053 unsecured debts listed in bankruptcy proceedings in Seattle, Washington, over a two-month period show the imprudence of this policy. Only 103 (9.8 percent) of the creditors involved had taken the trouble to obtain credit reports on their debt-ridden customers. Doctors, dentists and hospitals had the lowest incidence of checking: Only 1 percent of the medical accounts had bothered to investigate. Only 3 percent of auto-service firms were concerned enough to do any inquiring. The highest incidence of investigation was credited to department stores (42 percent) and finance companies (46 percent).

The survey disclosed that the credit grantors involved showed an incidence of checking that was substantially lower than the national average for their type of businesses. By failing to make an investigation, but by granting credit nevertheless, these retailers accelerated their customers' drift toward bankruptcy. In effect, they were a party to the loss they suffered.

A growing segment of merchants and retailers take very much a "so what" attitude toward statistics like these. They are concerned with doing volume business, and to encourage volume they pay little heed to credit information, accept low down payments and stretch installment payments over a long period of time. They feel that the amount of sales they will do as a result will more than make up for whatever financial losses they suffer. Some credit experts condemn this attitude. It means the retailer must tie up large sums of cash. Says one specialist: "Sometimes a fat order book can be a passport to disaster."

Some banks and small-loan companies lend money to individuals who might be considered marginal or even submarginal risks. Profit margins are the greatest when these businesses— like any others—operate at close to full capacity. When the manager of a bank or small-loan office must choose between greater profits and the increasing risk of loss, he invariably chooses the former. After all, any loss is tax deductible as a bad debt.

A lowering of credit standards is, of course, but one feature of the problem of overselling. When a hapless debtor is confronted with a fast-talking salesman, the match is hardly even. The salesman is interested in his commission, not in the fact that his prospective customer may be practicing budgetary brinkmanship. "These kinds of creditors *should* lose their money," says one bankruptcy referee.

Automobiles are probably oversold more than any other item. The credit manager of a large Los Angeles department store priced an automobile in the show window of a local dealer. He was told that it cost $4,600.

"How much should a man be earning in order to be able to buy such a car?" asked the credit man.

"Bankers tell me around $15,000 a year," the dealer answered.

"But who does buy them?"

"About 85 percent of them are sold to families with incomes of from $6,500 to $7,500 a year."

The dealer explained that he was under terrific pressure from the manufacturer to sell; in turn, he had to pressure his customers. Credit ratings? They hardly concerned him at all. He knew that if a customer became delinquent in his payments, he simply could repossess the automobile and get a deficiency judgment for the balance owed.

Bankruptcy referee Ray Kinnison of Los Angeles was asked why the number of bankruptcies in California is skyrocketing so. "The easy credit system is the main reason," he said. "No real credit check is being made."

Referee Kinnison explained that the "typical" person who files a petition is a wage earner who seeks to buy without a down payment. When he fills out an application for credit, he may list several references, but it is not likely they will be checked by the credit grantor. Credit investigations cost money, as much as $5 per applicant. Many businessmen prefer to set aside a fund to cover their credit losses and trust in the honesty of the customers who come to them. It costs no more than doing a thorough credit check, they figure.

The result is that the person who is hurrying toward a bankruptcy is seldom turned down in his quest for more and more credit. One day he finds that he owes "everyone in town." But when one creditor or a number of them begins legal action to collect, the debtor folds. In bankruptcy court he seeks refuge.

It is not likely that credit policies are going to change—at least not for some time. The press of competition is too great. "Sure we're against bankruptcy," says a department-store executive. "And we know getting tough on credit would help. The trouble is that no one wants to start. This is a competitive business. Either you compete or you get out."

CHAPTER 15

COLLECTION

In his best-selling book *Games People Play, The Psychology of Human Relationships,* Dr. Eric Berne writes of latter-day attitudes toward credit, debt and attempts at collection. "Try and Collect" is a game that is common among young married couples, he says. Participants buy all types of goods and services on credit, then fail to pay. The creditor begins collection procedures and the couple resist, enjoying not only the purchases but also what Dr. Berne calls "the pleasure of the chase." If the creditor gives up, the couple feels that they have won.

But if the creditor becomes aggressive in his collection efforts, it serves to strengthen the couple's will not to pay. And now the husband, having revealed the creditor as being greedy and ruthless, can disparage him to his friends. This gives him additional pleasure and also boosts his status. Further determined action by the creditor makes him appear increasingly despotic and grasping to the couple. "If that's the way creditors are," the couple reasons, "why pay anybody?"

All debtors are not as complacent and cunning as the people Dr. Berne describes. Nevertheless, failure to pay is a serious bit of business in every case, and credit grantors follow well-reasoned procedures to secure payment from delinquent accounts. Almost always the campaign follows the same pattern. At the beginning it is gentle, careful to preserve the good will of the customer. Gradually it builds in intensity, climaxing in legal action. In the final stages there is no "game" aspect to the confrontation. It is sheer warfare. And often bankruptcy is one of the spoils of the war.

Indeed, there is an extremely close relationship between collection activity and bankruptcy. Wherever very stringent collection laws exist, the per-capita rate of bankruptcy is very high, and vice versa. As this statement implies, there is no uniformity in collection laws. From state to state there is wide variance in the statutes concerning repossession, attachment and garnishment, the harshest methods of collection. As more than one observer has stated, this, in effect, means that the United States does not have "uniform laws on the subject of bankruptcies," as the Constitution dictates that it should have. We have a hodgepodge of systems instead.

The credit policies and the collection procedures that all credit grantors follow are closely linked. Every retailer and moneylender observes one of four modes of operation. They are: liberal credit and strict collection; strict credit and liberal collection; strict credit and strict collection; liberal credit and liberal collection.

The first two policies are those that the consumer encounters most often. Retail stores follow one or the other.

The third system—strict credit and strict collection—is characteristic of most personal finance companies, small-loan companies and commercial banks. The last named—liberal credit and liberal collection—is somewhat rare. Few business-men could follow such a policy and survive for very long.

Often collection policies vary somewhat in their intensity, depending on why credit was granted in the first place. Whether the retailer has a chattel mortgage is a significant factor. For

example, a petroleum company which has a delinquent account
for 300 gallons of fuel oil is going to be a great deal more
harsh in its collection techniques than a dealer who has lent
money on an automobile or a home freezer, hard goods that
are eminently repossessable.

But whether it involves an auto-loan payment, an installment
to the finance company or simply a bill from a local merchant
that is due beyond thirty days, the campaign begins as soon
as one's credit period expires. It is quite low-key and im-
personal in its initial stages. The creditor relies on the mails.
Copies of the bill bearing the outstanding charge or the
debtor's statement are sent. These may have a small sticker
affixed that declares "Please!" or "Past Due!" The relationship is still genial, for retailers realize that the great majority
of people with whom they are dealing have honestly overlooked the account and can be accused of no more than carelessness. Some are simply awaiting notice that it's time to
pay. A few may be short of funds.

When the first stage fails to provide payment, the campaign
gathers force. Now the letters—still form letters—reveal the
growing concern of the retailer. "Anything wrong?" they ask.
Or they have a "Tell-us-your-story" quality. Often at this junc-
ture the correspondence will seek to appeal to the customer's
sense of fair play or, by mentioning his credit responsibilities,
his pride.

It is now that the retailer attempts to establish why the
account is delinquent. Has the bill simply been overlooked?
Is the customer just being careless? Has he overbought or is
he short of cash? Has he been the victim of an accident? The
retailer wants to find out, and he begins to cannonade with
telephone calls, telegrams, special-delivery letters and certified
mail. If these efforts are unsuccessful, the crusade becomes
much more direct and personal. The retailer realizes that the

problem is grave and that he is probably dealing with some-one who disputes his claim, an insolvent or a customer who has no intention of paying.

Now the letters contain brusque demands. "Please remit by return mail or we shall have no alternative but to proceed further in this matter" is a standard method of appeal.

As a general rule, credit grantors are sympathetic toward those debtors who do have the courage to make contact with them and explain why their account is delinquent. "I don't mind waiting for my money if I know a person is in trouble," says a New York City dentist. "But why don't people just call and tell me?" Most retail outlets will allow a customer to skip a payment or two until he gets on solid ground again, then add those payments onto the end of the installment plan. Some-times they may suggest two or three months of token payments. Banks will often arrange for a loan to be refinanced. Sometimes smaller retailers will take back merchandise a customer has difficulty paying for.

The point is that most people fail to make contact with their creditors. Primarily, it is because they are embarrassed.

As a result, the situation steadily worsens. War clouds gather. The local credit bureau is advised of the debtor's im-prudent behavior. A letter may also go to the debtor's em-ployer. The telephone campaign is stepped up. Attempts are made to visit the debtor at his home. When a person will not answer his telephone or evades personal contact, the creditor may try to visit the "won't pay" in his home before or after work hours, say, at 7 A.M. or 10 P.M. The harassment is cease-less, and it can produce a high degree of nervous anxiety. Many a bankrupt person declares that "relief" is the foremost emotion they experience in going through a filing. One woman subjected to the pressures of collection recalls that "It almost drove me crazy. I got so that whenever I heard a car in the

driveway I would automatically take the children and even
the dog and head for a back bedroom."

The relationship between the debtor and his creditors at this
point is in the sharpest contrast to the amiability that existed
at the time the purchases were made. The understanding retailer who kindly offered to lower a down payment because
the debtor's credit rating was so high is now a man transformed. The "friendly banker" does not seem to have a good-
natured bone in his body.

Creditors have good reason for their growing and fearful
distress. The value of a past-due account falls off rapidly. The
Department of Commerce rates the value of accounts receivable this way:

DAYS PAST DUE	AVERAGE WORTH OF $1 OF ACCOUNTS RECEIVABLE
30 days	90 cents
6 months	67 cents
1 year	45 cents
2 years	23 cents
3 years	15 cents
5 years	1 cent

More and more retailers are turning to the professional
collection service to handle their delinquent accounts. Such
services operate as a department of a local credit bureau, or
they may be entirely separate. Either way, the collection service has one principal object: to recover money due. The storeowner pays the collection service on a commission basis out
of the money it collects. A prime reason for turning to the
collection agency is that it first investigates the delinquent account to establish why payment is not being made. Then it
tailors its collection methods to suit.

Collection services grade each problem account as being one of the four following types:

* The circumstantial debtor; this is the honest person who has been struck by misfortune, by an accident, a theft, or a loss of employment, and because of it is unable to meet his financial obligations. Such an individual is willing to do everything possible to pay his bills. Usually he requires financial advice and the time to regain his financial equilibrium.

* The mismanager; while inherently honest, this type of individual simply lacks the ability to budget his income and is too deeply in debt to pay. He too requires advice but also some prodding.

* The "won't pay"; this is the individual who has no intention of paying. He is experienced and adept at resisting or avoiding ordinary collection procedures and requires aggressive goading on the part of the collection agency.

* The "skip"; this is the "professional" debtor, the person who slips out of town after running up substantial bills at several stores. He leaves no evidence of where he is headed. Sometimes criminal prosecution must be resorted to in these cases.

Collection agencies employ the proper psychology, persistence and timing to deal with any set of circumstances. Not only are they likely to collect money which otherwise would be lost, but also they are sometimes able to transform a debtor into a good paying customer. But the fees that collection agencies charge are not small ones. They vary from one third to one half of the money collected, with the higher assessment for the unremunerative toil involved in collecting rent payments, accounts under $25 and ones that require litigation.

Though their collection activity may have proven futile, most large retailers and banks try to refrain from recourse to the courts whenever they can. One of a number of other courses of action may be possible.

For example, a department store may attempt to effect an extension agreement with a debtor who, for a valid reason— an accident or an unexpected financial reverse—is temporarily unable to make payment. An extension agreement simply gives the customer a greater length of time to meet his obligations. In the case of a thirty-day charge account, the extension is likely to involve the imposition of a service charge. Or the store may recommend that a thirty-day charge account be converted to a revolving charge account, with the attendant conditions and fees. If the balance due is large in relation to the debtor's income, the store may seek to convert the account to a series of notes, each with a due date and a carrying charge.

If an extension agreement is not feasible, sometimes a composition is. Under the terms of a composition each one of a group of creditors agrees to accept a reduced amount of their claims in settlement of the debt. A composition takes place, of course, only in the case of a debtor who is honest and conscionable. Usually it is a person whose indebtedness has been caused by a calamity or a period of adversity.

If such arrangements are not feasible and all attempts at collection have been in vain, legal proceedings begin. The good will of the customer is no longer of any concern. What precisely a creditor does at this stage often depends on the type of debt that exists. If it is a debt for hard goods, repossession is standard procedure. The creditor's right to retake a piece of property is usually found in the conditional sales contract and chattel-mortgage agreement. State laws set forth different conditions as to repossession, but usually all the creditor has to do is to show the court a possessory right superior to that of the debt. The court then grants a writ allowing the creditor to repossess.

In the majority of cases the first step a creditor takes is an attempt to have a judgment entered against the debtor. A

judgment is a court decision which substantiates the claim
and the amount. It is important to the creditor because it sets
the stage for further action.

The creditor obtains a judgment by bringing suit, usually
in municipal or civil court. Both parties appear and present
their cases. If the debtor (the defendant) does not appear in
court to answer the summons that he receives, the plaintiff is
granted a judgment by default. If the debtor does appear and
admits the debt—and more often than not the debtor has no
legal defense—the court renders a confession judgment.

In some states a debtor may give his creditor the power to
confess judgment for him should he fail to meet his payment
schedule. All the creditor has to do is appear in court to obtain the verifying order that the debt exists.

Judgments can be extremely costly to the debtor. Usually he
must bear all the plaintiff's legal fees, and these are added to
the amount he already owes. The debtor, though he often does
not realize it, agrees to pay such fees at the time he enters
into his contractual arrangement with the creditor. It is part of
the fine print of almost every sales contract or loan agreement.

For example, a loan applicant who seeks to do business with
the First National City Bank, which has its head office in New
York City, must agree that should he default in any one of his
installment payments, the entire note becomes due immediately.
The person in default must pay an attorney's fee to the bank
that amounts to fifteen percent of the note, and the various
costs and expenses the attorney incurs in the action as well.

The attorney's fee and all costs and expenses are items the
prospective borrower should view with some alarm. One customer of First National City Bank had an outstanding loan
balance of $1,790.71. He was unable to meet the payment
schedule and the bank obtained a default judgment against
him. But the amount of the judgment included not only the

money he owed the bank but also the attorney's fee the bank incurred, fines, interest, statute costs, a process fee, transcript and docking fees, and summons and complaint filing fees. The amount of the judgment entered was $2,167.11. The original amount had been swollen by more than 20 percent.

Another type of judgment familiar to many prospective bankrupts is the deficiency judgment. In essence it is the same as any other type of judgment; it is a verification by a court of money owed.

A deficiency judgment has to do with repossessed property, usually an automobile. When a debtor fails to make his payments, the creditor seizes the property involved. He then may resell the property or establish a fair value for it. Last, the creditor obtains a judgment for the difference between the resale price and the amount still owing—the deficiency. Hence the term "deficiency judgment." Again, all the costs for such action are borne by the creditor.

Deficiency judgments often play a meaningful role in bankruptcy proceedings. The customer is first surprised and then resentful when he learns that he must still pay for something that he no longer owns. "He's got his furniture. What more does he want?" the debtor reasons. With this attitude he does not have any qualms about filing a petition.

Another problem with deficiency judgments is that the property in question is often sold at less than fair market value. Why? Because the retailer does not have to drive a hard bargain in negotiating the sale. He knows the law obliges the debtor to pay whatever amount may still be owing.

In the poorer neighborhoods of many big cities repossession and the deficiency judgment have led to another type of shakedown. An unscrupulous retailer—a furniture dealer, say— enters into a working arrangement with a finance company. When the customer defaults, the finance company repossesses the merchandise. Then, as the law dictates, an auction sale is held to sell the goods. But at the auction the only one that shows up is the furniture dealer. He bids perhaps $30 for the furniture on which the debtor may still owe several hundred dollars. He must pay the deficiency even though the dealer has the furniture and may be able to sell it for a good price. The poor are made to operate in a "commercial jungle," says David Caplovitz of the Columbia University Bureau of Applied Research, "in which exploitation and fraud are the norm rather than the exception."

Another abuse involves the service of the summons which is meant to notify the debtor of the court hearing. In many neighborhoods the debtor never becomes aware of the hearing because the process server simply throws the summons away. The Harlem Consumer Education Council estimated that in some neighborhoods 95 to 99 percent of the summonses are never served. Because the server has been known to throw the summons down a sewer in such cases, this practice has come to be known as "sewer service." What happens, of course, is that a default judgment is entered against the debtor and he is not aware of it. Sometimes he gets his first indication he is in legal difficulty when the finance company backs up a big truck at his home or apartment to take away his furniture.

Sewer service could be checked if summonses were served hand to hand, with a signed receipt required, so attorneys for the Legal Aid Society in New York City declare. Also, they urge that it be made mandatory that a debtor be notified by certified mail before a default judgment can be entered against him.

Debtors who are the victims of practices like sewer service are willing candidates for bankruptcy, says Mrs. Florence Rice of the Harlem Consumer Education Council. "They feel that they have been duped—and they have been. Once someone tells them what bankruptcy is all about, they don't hesitate a minute about filing."

It is much more the exception than the rule, but there are some creditors who take little or no collection action. Professional moneylenders, such as local banks and small-loan companies, doggedly pursue whatever money is owed to them, utilizing every means of collection that state law will allow. The same is true of companies that operate on a national basis, and customarily extend credit in their operations.

The local retailer, however—a hardware store, a building-materials dealer or a neighborhood druggist—is not quite so determined in his collection procedures. Small businessmen are often of the idea that they should make their money at their calling, not in the pursuit of bad debts. Often they turn over their accounts receivable to a collection agency. While this can be costly, the fee paid is based on the amount of money collected, and using the collection agency enables the retailer to devote his full time to responsibilities he feels are more urgent.

Some manufacturing and service companies obtain credit insurance to protect themselves against poor credit risks, but such coverage is not available to insure retail credits, not yet anyway. Credit insurance simply involves paying a premium to an insurer, who assumes the problem of collection should the customer balk at paying his bills. Each policy has a deductible which is called the "primary less." According to J. L. McCauley, president of the American Credit Indemnity Company of New York, one of the two companies in the credit insurance business, "The deductible serves to make the policy holder a bit more cautious in granting credit because he assumes the first loss each policy year."

Mr. McCauley states that there is a public need for credit insurance on a retail level and that it is a "tremendous field."

But he says that standards haven't been developed yet which could allow insurers to undertake the risks involved.

Income-tax laws have come to be an important factor in collection, especially as they concern the local retailer. Bad debts are deductible as tax losses, and if the tax saving approximates the cost of collection, it is scarcely worthwhile pressing for payment.

Sometimes the collection methods mentioned in this chapter are to no avail. It is very often the case that the person headed for bankruptcy court has no assets whatsoever, nothing worth attaching or repossessing. But creditors have one other course of action—garnishment, the attachment of the debtor's wages. This is the subject of the next chapter.

CHAPTER 16

GARNISHMENT

Once a judgment has been entered against a debtor, garnishment proceedings are quite often the next step. The judgment substantiates that the debt exists; garnishment is the method of collecting it.

How garnishment affects the bankruptcy scene is the subject of great debate. Some people say that it is the foremost cause of bankruptcy filings.

Three states—Pennsylvania, Texas and Florida—forbid garnishment. Pennsylvania law grants ". . . the preservation to employees and their families of the fruits of mental or manual labor in order that their earnings may go to supply their daily needs without hindrance from their creditors." Texas law states simply: "No current wages for personal service shall ever be subject to garnishment."

But in the other forty-seven states several million workers have their wages garnished each year. Certain retailers and finance companies in each trading area specialize in this method of collection. Dr. Milton Huber, in his study of financially overextended families, found that in one Milwaukee county, of the 6,744 garnishments in one year, 805 of them were by one loan company, another 783 were by a credit clothing concern, and another 640 came from a credit appliance store.

Like the number of bankruptcies, the number of garnishments is growing. In Chicago, the Cook County Circuit Court issued 84,513 garnishments in 1965, 15 percent more than in 1964 and 72 percent more than in 1961. Garnishments in Los Angeles County are taking place at the rate of about 125,000 per year. Court officials in New York and Cleveland report rising totals of garnishments, too.

However, these figures for garnishments don't give a true picture of the amount of wage impounding. They don't include the number of wage assignments, and these accomplish for a creditor just what a garnishment does. A wage assignment is an agreement that a debtor enters into by which he pledges a portion of his wages to repay a debt should he default. Wage assignments are forbidden in only four jurisdictions—Alabama, the District of Columbia, Missouri and Ohio. The last-named forbids wage assignments unless they are for the support of the worker's family. A creditor prefers a wage assignment to a garnishment because the former does not involve getting a judgment against the debtor. It is virtually automatic.

The state of Ohio has somewhat softened the problem of garnishment with a trusteeship plan. Under this system, established by the state legislature, a worker pays a percentage of his earnings to a court and this money is prorated among his creditors. Garnishments are prohibited so long as the debtor makes regular payments to the trusteeship. In 1965 the Consumer Counseling Service of Cleveland handled approximately 3,200 trusteeships and disbursed $774,431 to creditors by means of this plan.

Sometimes a wage earner can prevent his salary from being garnished even though a creditor has obtained a judgment against him. He does this by means of an installment order, a device provided for under the laws of some states. To obtain such an order the debtor appears in court and requests that he be allowed to pay a part of the debt at a regular time over a specified period. Often the court determines the amount that must be paid. Once the installment order is granted, the court issues an injunction that prevents the judgment holder from initiating garnishment proceedings.

Often the amount that the wage earner must pay under the terms of the installment order is fixed by a schedule. For example, in the state of Michigan, if the amount of the judgment is less than $250, the amount of the payment must be $5 a week. A judgment of $500 requires a weekly payment of $10, and if the judgment is more than $500 the judge fixes the amount to be paid. If a debtor fails to meet the payment schedule, the creditor is allowed to bring garnishment proceedings.

Having a portion of one's wages seized is seldom less than a jarring experience, even to those to whom financial stress and creditor harassment is no particular novelty. Garnishment has not only caused people to file bankruptcy but also it has been blamed for triggering desertions, divorces and even suicides.

The fact that an employee can have a critical amount of money deducted from his pay check is not always the worst of it. Garnishment often causes a worker to lose his job. Employers say that such proceedings are expensive to them because they involve extra paper work and even court appearances. Many employers have a policy of dismissing any worker whose wages are garnished. Some permit one garnishment but no more. Others dismiss employees after two or three of them. A few companies will keep a man as long as he demonstrates that he is making a sincere effort to pay his debts.

There is one other way that garnishment does damage to a debtor. Often it is like a signal flare to his other creditors, an indication to them that danger lies ahead. Immediately a crush of other collection activity begins.

State statutes concerning garnishment vary widely. In some states the creditor must obtain a judgment before he can impose his attachment, but most states permit the creditor to garnishee when he initiates his suit. Some states make it mandatory that the creditor impose a separate levy each pay day. In others the initial order remains in effect until the debt is satisfied.

All of the states that permit garnishment exempt some portion of the debtor's wages from attachment, but the amount of these exemptions covers a considerable range. Some states express their exemptions in dollar amounts. These vary from a mere $35 a week in North Dakota to $350 a month for married debtors and $200 for single debtors in Alaska. In other states exemptions are given in percentages. They range from only 50 percent of one's earnings in Arizona, Oregon and California to as much as 100 percent in North Carolina, South Carolina and South Dakota.

There is a very definite relationship between the number of bankruptcy filings in a state and the character of that state's wage-exemption statutes. In states where wage exemptions are so high as to give little meaning to garnishment as a collection device, few bankruptcies occur; but in states where exemptions are low, the number of bankruptcies per capita is high. Solid evidence supports this:

STATE	NUMBER OF BANKRUPTCIES PER 100,000 POPULATION (FISCAL 1967)
"High" Exemptions	
Texas	5
Pennsylvania	9
Florida	19
North Carolina	5
"Low" Exemptions	
California	197
Washington	154
Ohio	178
Oregon	246

Many bankruptcy referees testify to the validity of what these statistics imply. Estes Snedecor, referee in bankruptcy in Portland, Oregon, and a member of the Advisory Committee on General Orders in Bankruptcy appointed by the Chief Justice of the United States, declares that "The underlying causes of personal or consumer bankruptcy are: unemployment, over-extension of credit, deficiency claims arising from repossessions of automobiles and appliances sold on contract, excessive interest rates and unusual medical and hospital bills, but the one overriding cause precipitating consumer bankruptcies is the garnishment or threat of garnishment of wages coupled with unrealistic wage exemptions." Referee Snedecor told a House Banking Subcommittee, which was taking testimony on the credit disclosure bill, that many bankrupts "come to me after court is over to say that they would have been able to pay their bills if they had been given the opportunity, but repeated garnishments had prevented them from holding steady jobs."

Referee Clive Bare of Knoxville, Tennessee, who has handled more than 10,000 bankruptcy cases in the past ten years, says that from 60 to 70 percent of the filings were a direct result of wage garnishments. "Many individuals are being driven into bankruptcy who actually owe relatively small sums —but whose wages are under attachment," says Referee Bare. "They are financially overextended, but if given an opportunity to pay their debts could do so within a reasonable period of time."

In Tennessee, prior to July 1, 1967, only $17 per week of a wage earner's salary was exempt from garnishment, plus $2.50 a week for each dependent child. A new statute became effective on July 1, 1967, which raised the exemption to 50 percent or $20 a week, whichever is greater, with a maximum total exemption of $50 a week. The $2.50 additional exemption for each child was not changed. Thus, the head of a family with four dependent children who earns $60 a week has $40 a week exempt from attachment, giving him an annual income of $4,080, well below the established "poverty" level.

Los Angeles bankruptcy referee Ronald Walker says that garnishment puts a "big burden" on large companies because it complicates their bookkeeping and because garnished employees cannot do their work properly. "A lot of big companies have a limit of two attachments and then the employee is fired," Referee Walker points out. "So people go bankrupt as a form of job insurance."

Garnishment has also proven to be a particularly severe method of dealing with the poor class of debtor. Says Mrs. Florence Rice, head of the Harlem Consumer Education Council, "Many of the desertion cases we hear about are garnishee desertions. When a man's salary is impounded, he may not be able to support his family on the money that is left. He deserts and the family goes on welfare."

David Caplovitz of the Bureau of Applied Research of Columbia University says that families can *become* poor through difficulties presented by such as wage attachments. "To lose a job because of a garnishment is certainly one way of entering the ranks of the impoverished," he states.

Organized labor has likened the practice of firing a debt-burdened worker to the seventeenth-century custom of locking debtors in prison. Union officials have been campaigning diligently in recent years to soften state exemption laws, urging legislators to increase the amount of wages exempt from garnishment. These efforts have met with success in about a dozen states.

Another union goal is to put a ban on the firing of any employee whose wages have been garnished. Early in 1967 the state of New York passed a law which prevents an employer from firing a debtor if there is only one garnishment against his salary. However, with the second garnishment the employer could fire the man with impunity.

Some lawmakers have come to look on garnishment as wholly evil and seek to legislate it out of existence. Representative Leonor K. Sullivan of Missouri wrote a ban on garnishment into the House version of the Senate-passed interest disclosure bill. A panel of bankruptcy referees testified before a subcommittee of the House and tended to support Mrs. Sullivan's efforts. Undoubtedly such a law would stem the rising tide of bankruptcies, but it would also produce a whole new catalog of credit ills.

The problems that could conceivably arise have been discerned by David R. Earl, a member of the board of directors of the American Collectors Association and author of *The Bankruptians*, a critical study of latter-day bankruptcy practices. Mr. Earl agrees that states like Texas, Florida and North Carolina—that is, states where wage garnishments are scarcely permitted and which have collection laws he calls "weak"—cannot, in law, force a debtor to pay. In these states creditors are not able to cause debtors more than "a slight inconvenience." It follows that these states have a low per-capita number of bankruptcies. There is simply no necessity to file.

However, these states have higher credit losses and more mortgage foreclosures than what is normal. And it is also true that charge-account customers and home mortgagors pay better in states that have the most bankruptcies per capita. When the consumer knows that he can be harassed—legally—to pay a just debt, he feels a much stronger commitment to meet his obligations.

Mr. Earl points to two of the states where garnishments are not permitted—Texas and Florida—and notes that they lead all other states in the number of FHA mortgage defaults. And he says that collection agencies in these two states are able to liquidate only one third as much as the national average for their profession.

A survey by the Bankruptcy Study Committee of the American Collectors Association showed that states with high per-capita rates of bankruptcy are not necessarily states that are suffering any economic distress. Indeed, quite the opposite is true, the ACA report demonstrated. When collection laws are "strong"—that is, where garnishment is lawful and statutes exempt a relatively small portion of the worker's income and where attachment and repossession are permitted—credit losses are kept extremely low. As a result, in these states the cost of credit is low, too.

The ACA studied accounting records of several national retailers, comparing the number of customer defaults in states with high and low per-capita rates of bankruptcy. The study revealed that "losses in low bankruptcy states are 50 percent greater than in high per capita bankruptcy states."

As an example, the ACA showed the relationship between bad debt charge-offs for Ohio, which ranked ninth in the number of bankruptcies per capita in 1966, and Delaware, which ranked forty-fourth. The median income for both states was virtually the same. Delaware, said the ACA, showed a credit grantor loss four times greater than Ohio over the three years analyzed.

What really distresses the ACA are the people who extol the low per-capita number of bankruptcies in those states that have no garnishment and weak collection laws. Mr. Earl draws this analogy. "Suppose," he says, "that we relaxed our traffic laws in such a manner that few arrests were made for driving violations." The number of accidents could conceivably swell to macabre proportions. "Should we then point with pride to the arrest record," he asks, "and claim it is proof that the traffic problem has been solved and that people have become better drivers?" He states that the high incidence of bank-ruptcy can no more be attributed to energetic collection activi-ties than our growing crime rate can be said to be caused by diligent law enforcement.

This is a valid argument. To abolish garnishment would merely be to exchange one set of problems for another. A bet-ter solution would be to bring all state exemptions to realistic levels. A debtor should not be able to be deprived of so much of his income that the welfare of his family is in any way jeopardized, yet creditors should be armed with some garnish-ment statute in their siege against delinquent accounts. A "middle area" must be found, equitable to both parties, and be made uniform for the entire country.

David Caplovitz, in testifying before the Subcommittee on Consumer Affairs of the House Committee on Banking and Currency, declared that he is "not convinced" that doing away with garnishment would have the desired effects. Said Caplo-vitz, "Garnishment is not permitted in Pennsylvania and yet credit merchants are thriving in that state and consumer fraud is just as prevalent there as elsewhere. The creditors in Penn-sylvania do not hesitate to attach both personal and real prop-erty and sheriff's sales of furniture and even homes are quite common."

The Uniform Consumer Credit Code, now being drafted by the National Conference of Commissioners on Uniform State Laws, would set exemptions at $100 per week for debtors with dependents and $65 a week for others, though it would limit this protection to consumer credit claims.

Even if garnishment were banned, the impounding of wages would still be possible. Creditors in many states would in no way be prevented from levying against a worker's salary by means of a wage assignment. The same cycle would develop.

There would be a spell of overbuying, with the debtor eventually being driven into bankruptcy court with the idea of freeing his wages from creditor claim.

The Consumer Credit Protection Act of 1968 exempted a mere 25 percent of an employee's take-home pay. It also exempted a minimum of $48 in weekly take-home pay.

Referee Lawrence Miller of the Northern District of Illinois, Eastern Division, suggests that an 85 to 90 percent exemption is a fair one. An exemption of 90 percent means that a worker who is earning $125 a week and is garnished has his weekly earnings reduced to $113, certainly not a level that implies hardship. A 90 percent exemption would surely take much of the terror out of garnishment proceedings in states like Ohio and Oregon, and thereby work to reduce the number of bankruptcy filings. And by moderating the amount of money being collected, it would make retailers and moneylenders a bit more judicious in extending credit to those people who are already shouldering a heavy debt load.

CHAPTER 17

DEBT
COUNSELING

Almost without exception the person who is heavily in debt and a likely candidate for bankruptcy can be saved from that fate —if he gets help. Before his financial tangle becomes hopeless he needs to have someone take an objective look at his situation and set a course for him to follow out of the wilderness.

Such counsel may not yet be easily available, but a candle has been lighted in the darkness in the form of the many advice-giving agencies in the field of money management that have been established in the past decade. At the end of 1967 fifty communities in the United States and Canada were offering counsel in handling credit and paying debts, and at least that many other cities were considering the founding of such agencies. Most such services are centered in the Mideast, although almost a dozen have been established in California in recent years. The fewest number are in the Northeast. All in all, the emergence of the community-based credit-counseling program is one of the most significant advances in the credit field in recent years.

The motivation here is not altruistic. The fact that more than a billion dollars a year is being washed down the drain through personal bankruptcy is the prime factor. The credit community is alarmed. In most cases where counseling agencies have been established it is the finance companies, local retailers and banks—the credit grantors—who have been the prime movers.

While the basic idea of these counseling agencies is to provide immediate assistance to those overburdened with debt, businessmen hope that these agencies will eventually help to change the attitude of some consumers toward money owed. "There are some people who have to develop a more meaningful responsibility."

The National Foundation for Consumer Credit, a trade association for small-loan companies, merchants and some banks, and an organization that sponsors research and education in consumer credit, has assisted in the establishment of about two thirds of the country's counseling agencies. Those established with the help of the NFCC adopt the name "Consumer Credit Counseling Service of (name of city)," and they are permitted to use the NFCC's copyrighted insigne.

Both the NFCC (1411 K Street N.W., Washington, D.C.) and the International Credit Association (375 Jackson Avenue, St. Louis, Missouri) offer staff assistance and information kits to community groups interested in establishing non-profit credit-counseling agencies. Other organizations striving to promote the idea of community credit counseling are the Associated Credit Bureaus of America and the National Consumer Finance Association, trade association for small-loan companies.

Family credit counseling is neither new nor unique. To some degree it has been practiced ever since the late Henry Ford began to offer his horseless carriage to the American public at so much down and so much a week.

Social agencies, Legal Aid societies and some labor unions

have a tradition of helping people manage their finances. Lawyers and bankers help. Many credit bureaus have some type of advice-giving service, and some have specially trained personnel who give counsel. Many credit unions offer financial advice. Usually it is provided by the credit-union officers or committees, but in recent years some credit unions have hired full-time counselors.

Some credit grantors, principally consumer finance companies, offer counseling service, however self-serving this function might be. The manager or owner of a finance company might suggest an adjusted payment schedule to a debtor family. In some cases he will contact other creditors involved in an effort to persuade them to accept the plan.

Various family service agencies provide assistance in money management, too. In recent years the Office of Economic Opportunity has seen the need for financial counseling. At first the OEO sought to aid debt-ridden families with just legal assistance, but beginning in 1966 the agency put into operation family debt counseling centers in Phoenix, Minneapolis and Oakland County, Michigan (Royal Oak and Pontiac).

The pioneer agency in credit counseling was established in 1955 by the Capital Finance Corporation of Columbus, Ohio. It was known as the Economy Budget Service Company and it operated in connection with a branch office of the finance company. But demand proved so great—an average of fifty debtors a month were applying for service—that it soon became necessary to rent space in another building. Two counselors were employed, both former employees of the loan company.

As detailed by Harry E. Fuller, vice-president of the Capital Finance Corporation, the first step in consumer counseling is to obtain an itemized list of all the debtor's creditors and the amount owed to each. The debtor provides this. Then each debt is verified with the appropriate creditor. Next a complete and accurate listing of the debtor's living expenses is compiled. His income completes the picture.

Then the counselor evolves a budget for the debtor, and he telephones each creditor and advises him of the plan for rehabilitation. Last, the debtor turns over to the counselor the agreed-on sum each pay day, and this money is disbursed to the creditors.

When the applicant fails to make a payment, he is immediately contacted by the counselor and impressed with the importance of keeping to the payment schedule. If, either through disinterest or carelessness or both, the debtor persists in his delinquency, the case is dropped and the creditors are so notified.

In its first six years of operation Economy Budget had a total of 4,078 people inquire about its service. Some of these needed no more than a "pep talk," says Mr. Fuller, someone to encourage them to pay their debts by pointing up the penalties for delinquency. Others only needed advice, perhaps the recommendation that they contact a creditor and work out an extension agreement. A total of 761 people, about 35 percent of those counseled, were actually budgeted by the service— that is, they had their debts consolidated and were put on an eighteen- to twenty-four-month payment plan.

Approximately 30 percent of those budgeted were faithful to the payment schedule to the very end. Importantly, of the 761 people who began the payment plan, only twenty-seven, or 4.3 percent, eventually filed bankruptcy, and only five, or 1 percent of the total, took refuge in Ohio's trusteeship statutes. Says Mr. Fuller: "I have no way of proving this, but I suspect a considerable number of 761 prorate cases, as well as many of the others we counseled, would have ended up in bankruptcy had we not helped them. Not only did the debt-ridden benefit. Each year approximately 200 retailers in the

Columbus area—stores, hospitals, credit unions, banks, finance companies and doctors and lawyers—received payment as a result of the service."

As Harry Fuller's experience suggests, credit counseling agencies do much more than just counsel. Their principal function is to develop a debt payment plan for each person interviewed.

A typical client is the twenty-nine-year-old shoe salesman who sought assistance from the Community Credit Counseling Service of Greater Atlanta. He had accumulated a debt load of $5,300, mostly because he had purchased two automobiles and borrowed from small-loan companies. He and his wife, a high-school instructor in music, had a monthly take-home income of $568, but their monthly installment payments were $316. The balance—$252—was not enough to cover living expenses for them and their two children.

Creditors had begun to contact the couple's employers, and the wife faced the loss of her job. In the circumstances this would have meant disaster. But the agency's counselor worked out a plan that called for payments of $270 a month. Each of the salesman's creditors approved the plan. Then twice a month he delivered $135 in cash to the counseling service. In less than two years he planned to be debt-free for the first time in his marriage.

The association between the agency and the debtor begins with what is called a "work-up" interview. Both the counselor and debtor try to acquire a realistic view of the family's expenses. Are food costs out of line? Can an insurance premium or two be skipped without a lapse in coverage? Can auto expenses be reduced? Is the telephone a necessity? The counselor seeks to increase the family's income by encouraging the husband to work overtime. Other members of the family are asked to seek part-time employment.

The outflow of money has to be checked. The counselor tries to arrange extensions and consolidations on installment notes. In the case of a loan, he attempts to have the co-signer take over payments. He suggests the family trade in their car for a less expensive model with the idea of lowering the auto payments or doing away with them. He recommends less expensive living quarters.

Not everyone who seeks help from a counseling service is accepted. Not by any means. In some cases the debt load is simply too massive. There is no reasonable solution to the problem. Sometimes the repayment plan as developed by the agency is rejected by the individual or family because it involves too much sacrifice. Other times families are not accepted because of "problems beyond the scope of the agency." This usually refers to marital difficulties.

Clients who are accepted for counseling are made to realize that the responsibility for success of the program rests with them and that getting out of debt is not an easy matter. "You are the only one who can get yourself out of debt," a brochure from Family Debt Counselors of Phoenix tells prospective clients. "It will not be quick or easy . . . there is a long, tough road ahead. It certainly will mean foregoing any new purchases, exercising much self-restraint, getting by with less and making things do."

Usually counseling agencies are financially supported by the creditors of a community. Finance companies, retailers and banks are solicited for funds each year. In some cases, part of the operating expenses comes from fees that are charged clients. The subject of fees is a controversial subject. Some counselors feel that when an agency begins to collect service charges it loses its "community-sponsored" image. It begins to look as if profit is a concern and people grow suspicious of it, particularly if the service is promoted by the

community's credit grantors. There is also the argument that
the people the agency wants to attract are the very ones least
able to pay. Any fee is a burden, however small.

Other counselors feel that applicants should be asked to pay
nominal fees. "When people get something for nothing, they
don't appreciate it," says one counselor. "Sometimes they are
suspicious. Besides, the fee helps to preserve the debtor's self-
respect. He doesn't feel that he's taking a handout."

The Family Debt Counselors of Phoenix, one of the first
community counseling services to be established, charges a fee
of $2 a month to those clients whose debts it consolidates and
budgets. It also charges a $1 application fee; however, in genu-
ine hardship cases no fees of any type are assessed. In many
cities counseling services are prohibited from charging fees
by local or state statutes.

Reports from various counseling agencies indicate the
notable successes that have been achieved.

* The Family Debt Counselors of Phoenix, founded in
1955, was the first counseling agency to be sponsored as a
community-service activity, not simply as a subsidiary of a
credit grantor or loan company. The increasing number of
bankruptcies plus damage done by commercial debt consolidators were the two basic reasons the agency was founded. Local
retailers were quick to support the service. It grew to become
an organization of approximately 75 volunteer counselors. It
averages about $600,000 annually in disbursements to credi-
tors. Local businessmen bear a major share of the expenses.

* The Consumer Credit Counseling Service of Metropolitan
Cleveland has a membership of 73 business firms. Service
began in November 1964 and has gradually expanded since
that time. The agency paid creditors $257,330 during 1966.

* The Michigan League Budget Service, Inc., a subsidiary
of the Michigan Credit Union League, began operation in 1961
to provide budget counseling service to credit-union members,

but in May 1965 its services were extended to the general public. It has its principal office in Detroit and branch offices in Benton Harbor, Ecorse, Flint, Lansing, Royal Oak, Saginaw and Wayne. In Detroit between 200 and 250 new families seek the agency's help each month. During the first six months of 1966 a total of $965,710 was paid to creditors. Families using the service pay a fee of $3 a week.

* Chicago's service, known as the Family Financial Counseling Service of Greater Chicago, began operation in 1965. Besides advising clients and budgeting their payments, the agency has been credited with extricating some of its applicants from the clutches of local loan sharks.

* The Consumer Credit Counseling Service of Greater Atlanta, Inc., boasts a board of directors that broadly represents Atlanta's credit grantors and also includes representatives of the Better Business Bureau and the legal community. The Atlanta Consumer Credit Association founded the service in 1961, mainly out of concern about the drastic increase in the number of bankruptcies. During August 1966, a fairly typical month, the Atlanta agency counseled 132 new applicants, and prorate service was begun with 94 of them, bringing to 458 the number of active prorate accounts. A total of $49,892 in payments went to creditors that month.

Small cities, too, have obtained noteworthy results from debt counseling. Goshen, Indiana, with a population of approximately 15,000, distributes more than $5,000 a month to creditors by means of a CCC service.

Charleston, West Virginia, South Bend, Indianapolis, Salt Lake City, Spokane, Newark and Philadelphia are other cities that have established counseling services in recent years. In California, counseling agencies have been established in San Diego, Sacramento, Oakland, San Jose, Kern County and Ventura County.

The spiraling number of bankruptcies is the reason for this

activity. In 1966 California had 34,255 personal bankruptcies, 18 percent of the national total. Counseling may be helpful in reversing the trend. The city of Sacramento established a community counseling service in 1964. That year the amount of money lost to creditors through personal bankruptcy was approximately $7 million in the Sacramento area. But in 1965 the figure decreased to $4.3 million, though bankruptcy losses in nearby areas continued their upward rise, increasing by 7 percent. The counseling staff in Sacramento believes that they have "saved" 65 percent of the people who were headed for bankruptcy from filing.

Early in 1967 the business and financial leaders of Los Angeles announced plans to establish community counseling in that city. The board of directors of the newly formed agency included presidents, vice-presidents and credit managers of some of the largest business and financial groups in the state.

As stated by Walter Bruner, chairman of the State of California Counselors, the first aim is to foster education in the use of credit and to pinpoint the dangers of overbuying. The second is to help those most heavily in debt to work out a plan to pay their bills.

The Los Angeles agency was to be financed from voluntary contributions from business and financial institutions. It was to be a "true public service." About $60,000 was anticipated as being necessary for the first year's expenses. But no fees were to be charged to debtor-applicants.

Chairman Bruner declares that the idea of a counseling service makes sense "from an arithmetical standpoint." He says that "Even if a business were to pay 10 percent of all the money collected for it by the counseling service, it would be cheaper than paying heavy collection costs."

The Los Angeles agency does not expect to limit its services solely to those who seek advice on debt management. Plans include arranging classes in home economics for young couples and providing speakers for local clubs and high schools. And sellers as well as buyers, any firm which lends money or extends credit, would be offered information to help reduce losses.

Debit counseling is also performed on a commercial basis, by individuals or firms that offer their services for a fee to those in debt trouble. This aspect of counseling is bitterly controversial.

There are approximately 300 commercial counseling offices in operation today, most of them in the industrial cities of the Midwest. There are some on the Pacific Coast but hardly any at all in the East. State laws or city ordinances set license requirements for these agencies and determine what fees they can charge. In almost all of the Eastern Seaboard states, commercial credit counseling has been defined as constituting the practice of law and thus has been effectively banned. Interestingly, such statutes have resulted from diligent and fervent lobbying on the part of credit grantors, particularly small-loan companies, not from pressure exerted by the legal profession.

The typical commercial counselor gained his experience with a small-loan company, a bank or a credit union. He operates an office with three to six employees, and he may service as many as 250 to 500 clients at one time. Often he is referred to as a debt consolidator, pooler or adjuster, though in most cases these are terms of opprobrium. He may or may not consolidate a client's debts. In most legitimate operations he does not.

A commercial adjuster begins by interviewing the debtor, and then, if he feels that the debtor has the earning capacity to pay, he sets up a budget for him to follow and notifies his creditors of the payment plan. He sees to it that the debtor adheres to the payment schedule and counsels him as new problems develop.

Seemingly this is a sound practice, yet debt counseling has

come in for sharp criticism in the past decade, particularly along the Eastern Seaboard. Such operations have been accused of incompetence, lack of principle and flagrant dishonesty. Some of the criticism is justified. Unfortunately, the unscrupulous practices of some commercial counselors have blackened the image of the counseling field in general in many sections of the country.

The matter of fees is one area of abuse. Consumer Credit specialists say that in some instances the costs imposed by the debt consolidator are excessive, that the already overburdened debtor simply cannot afford the additional expenses that may amount to 10 or 15 percent of the money he already owes. Instead of doing anything constructive about his indebtedness, the debtor is simply adding another creditor to a list already too long. New York Attorney General Louis Lefkowitz, warning consumers late in 1967 that debt pooling was "on the rise" again, declared that the debtor who gets involved in a debt-pooling scheme "is worse off than when he started. He is saddled with high interest charges, service charges and other costs."

There is more than one case of completely fraudulent fees being charged. The Washington *Evening Star* exposed the dishonest practices of some debt consolidators in a series of articles early in 1967 and disclosed that New Orleans had some debt poolers charging their clients between 40 and 50 percent annual interest on the unpaid balance of their indebtedness, plus a $17 monthly service charge.

Misleading advertising is another practice of which professional consolidators have been accused, and some are guilty of the charge. They solicit business by postcard and letter, building mailing lists from court records of people being sued for debt or from street-address directories. "We understand that you are having problems with your bills," declares a typical postcard message. "We wonder if we can help." A telephone number is given, and a high-powered salesman is ready to answer the call.

Other commercial debt adjusters use radio, television or the newspapers. A typical advertisement proclaims: "One simple easy weekly payment pays all your debts." Another says: "If you owe $1,000, pay as little as $15 a week." A third declares: "Save worry and your credit standing; stop garnishments, repossessions and lawsuits."

The advertisements attempt to establish the impression that the consolidator will lend the debtor money to pay all his bills and that he will be immediately relieved from the pressure being exerted by creditors. Both impressions are false. Debt adjusters seldom lend money or even advance a single payment, and they have no more power than the debtor himself to forestall garnishments, repossessions and the like. Relief from collection action can come only with the consent of the creditor. The adjuster serves as no more than a hired agent of the debtor, who continues to owe each of his creditors individually. The adjuster merely apportions funds to each of them.

Some commercial proraters do provide additional funds for their clients, and in such cases sky-high interest rates have been charged. A middle-aged Laurel, Maryland, homeowner, behind in his installment payments, consulted a local debt adjuster in an effort to obtain $1,260 he needed to pay his creditors. Under the agreement he entered into he converted the $1,260 debt into a $4,000 second mortgage on his home. "And he was still broke," said Randolph Hughes, Maryland State Banking Commissioner.

A Wilmington, Delaware, man, with a steady job and the owner of a $22,000 home with a $12,000 first mortgage, sought help from a commercial prorater to pay off an auto loan and some other debts. They totaled $2,600. The adjuster said he would provide the money. "I signed about eight papers," the man told the local Better Business Bureau later. "I didn't know what I was signing. There were so many it would have taken me a week to read them." A few weeks later the man received an installment payment book from a Philadelphia loan company. It called for sixty payments of $87.40 each—a total of $5,244. "I couldn't find out what the extra $2,600 was for," the man complained. "What did they pull on me?" One Delaware attorney called such proraters "legal loan sharks."

The most serious accusation is that debt consolidators have been known to pocket the funds of their clients. A seventeen-year-old Washington, D.C., couple, newly married and heavily in debt for furniture, went to a commercial consolidator with the idea that he would pay off all their bills and then they would pay him in small installments. Each week they sent the adjuster a $31 money order. At the end of two months they began to get phone calls and letters from everyone they owed. "Don't worry," the young man told his creditors. "I've paid the adjuster; he'll pay you." The couple were awakened to the realities of the situation when the bride's mother, who had guaranteed the couple's auto loan because they were minors, was told her salary was about to be garnished if she didn't make a payment on the car right away. The adjuster had not made a single one.

No less than twenty-two states now prohibit charging a debtor for counseling, and thirteen other states have passed licensing and regulatory legislation. The most determined of the debt poolers have found ways to circumvent the laws, however. For example, Rhode Island is one of the states that has banned consolidators, yet several such operations are still based in the state, using the mails to function and soliciting clients from every state—except Rhode Island. Not long ago the city of Baltimore passed a law prohibiting debt poolers only to see several of them set up shop outside the city limits and continue in their quest for clients among Baltimore's residents.

There can be no doubt about it—there is deception and dishonesty in the credit counseling field. Even the American Association of Credit Counselors, an organization of about fifty adjusters, admits to the existence of "the *bad* credit counselor—the lazy, the incompetent, the dishonest."

The AACC explains that there are a number of ways in which one can single out the legitimate counselor from the unprincipled one. The fee charged by an honest counselor will be no more than $8 to $12 a month, and he will not accept any money until the payment plan is worked out. He will develop a realistic payment schedule for the debtor and provide him with a written statement of all charges, terms and a list of the accounts to be paid. He will make payments promptly. He will not engage in misleading advertising or encourage bankruptcy proceedings. He will make a conscientious effort to have each program brought to a successful conclusion.

The very best way for a debtor to check on the standing of a debt counseling agency is simply to consult his creditors about it. If they downgrade the adjuster, it is not likely he will be able to offer any meaningful assistance.

AACC officials say that most of the censure heaped on commercial counselors comes from creditors. "They don't want us around," says L. M. Finley, president of Debt Reducers, a successful and respected counseling agency in Portland, Oregon. "They fear the loss of control our presence gives them. They're not in a position to direct the debtor; they have to accept what the counselor allots them. That's why they don't like us.

"Naturally, we charge the debtor," states Mr. Finley. "He

should be charged. He expects it. How can anyone work for him without charging him? And unless the debtor has some financial commitment to the plan, he has little desire to make it a success."

To sum up, some commercial counselors are fine and upstanding. Some, particularly in the East, are anything but. However, the dishonest ones have been guilty of such an array of unprincipled practices that they have awakened consumer watch-dog agencies and even law-enforcement officials to their existence. Because of the attention they have attracted, and because of the laws many states have enacted setting operational standards and procedures, it is difficult nowadays for a commercial counselor to operate unethically and stay in business for very long.

Unfortunately, the stigma attached to some commercial debt consolidators has carried over to the community counseling service. When a community agency sought to establish itself in Baltimore, the support it might have received was diminished by the bad effects that had been wrought by unscrupulous debt poolers. In general, the field has an imperfect image, but as community credit counseling becomes more widespread, the distortions are being corrected.

Community debt counseling services work to the benefit of everyone involved. They help the debtor by giving him the counsel he needs so desperately. In his chagrin at owing, the average debtor seeks to avoid his creditors, and this compounds the problem. The angered creditors begin to take drastic action—they repossess; they garnish. The reason that creditors hail debt counseling is no mystery: They receive the money that is due them and without having to institute legal action.

Of course, it is not just enough to offer a counseling service. It has to be carefully planned so as to conform to the attitudes and habits of those it means to counsel. Dr. Milton J. Huber, in attempting to locate cooperative interviewees for his study of the overextended family, found that ". . . many couples are more reluctant to discuss their finances than their sexual problems in marriage." Counseling offices have to be strategically placed. And the availability of the service must get appropriate attention through the press, radio and television, especially the last-named.

Families in slum areas are a special problem as far as counseling is concerned. They have few dealings with banks or credit unions and other advice-giving agencies. Their friends and co-workers are as uninformed about credit and debt as they are.

In his study *The Poor Pay More*, David Caplovitz found that low-income families found it difficult to get to the public and private agencies best equipped to help them. Often the agencies were located a considerable distance from the consumer's homes or their services were available only during the hours the consumers were at work. One of Caplovitz's suggestions was that counselors seek to imitate the peddler practice of calling on families in their homes in an attempt to reach them before they became overburdened with consumer problems. "This would only be emulating some enterprising merchants . . ." says Caplovitz.

Indeed, in the case of low-income families and those whose income is not so low, emphasis should be placed on getting to the debtor early, before the problem has become acute. Financial difficulties are something like medical ills—the earlier they are detected, the less painful the remedy and the more permanent the cure.

CHAPTER **18**

SOME
CONCLUSIONS

Consumer bankruptcies are multiplying, a fact that one's daily newspaper will probably affirm. They have swelled from a mere 8,500 in 1946 to close to 192,000 in 1967.

Despite this rather spectacular increase in number and the fact that these bankruptcies wash out well over a billion dollars a year in indebtedness, they have yet to have a distinctly harmful effect on the nation's economy. There is not a single case of a retailer's business bankruptcy being caused by the prior bankruptcy of his customers. The loss rates of banks and small-loan companies are not high. Seldom are they more than 1 percent. Nevertheless, it would not be wise to ignore what is happening on the bankruptcy scene. The storm is gathering. The nation's economic health is helplessly dependent on credit and payment. Should denial of debt and default become pandemic, should long lines begin to form outside the bankruptcy courts of the land, the results would be ruinous.

Too many purported solutions to the bankruptcy problem concentrate solely on decreasing losses to creditors. This is important, of course, but the problem is much broader. Debt—heavy debt—is the main topic, and bankruptcy is only one manifestation of it.

Psychiatrists agree that indebtedness and the pressures that accompany it—the loss of self-respect, the scorn—are reflected in many ways, in family disintegration and even suicide. Debt can be the cause of crime and abandonment. And just plain grief.

It goes without saying that there are going to be families in debt trouble as long as credit is available. But the number of families in crisis situations can be reduced, and one way to do it is through education, not merely consumer education as it is now practiced but by means of formal instruction in high schools in family budgeting, buymanship and the use of credit. These subjects should be made mandatory for all youngsters, boys and girls, college preparatory students and vocational trainees.

In many cases money today is easier to earn than it is to manage, and it is unrealistic that an individual devote years to preparing himself for a good paying job but scarcely any time at all to the use and management of what he plans to earn.

"Young people today don't know what credit really is," says Lew Finley, head of a Portland, Oregon, credit counseling firm. "They've never had a course in economics or household budgeting. No one has ever told them what money is all about." Many young people today never stop to realize that the high standard of living they enjoy is partly a result of perhaps a decade or more of diligent saving and some self-denial on the part of their parents. Indeed it is the young people who need instructional aid the most. Every study ever prepared shows that it is the young families that are the ones that are most bankruptcy prone.

Late in 1967 the Family Service Association of America completed a survey of family credit counseling in the United States, as provided through non-profit community-based programs. One aspect of the study focused on sixty-five families who had availed themselves of counseling service— that is, families with a critical amount of debt.

"These families are young," the report concluded. In two thirds of the families the age of the breadwinner was thirty to thirty-five. There were two to three children per family. The husbands held "blue collar" jobs and one of every four wives also worked. Family debt ranged from $2,000 to over $8,500. What brought them into debt trouble? Unsophisticated shopping habits, compulsive buying and low sales resistance—what the Family Service Association characterized as "poor judgment."

"It seems that all teen-age boys think about today is owning their own cars," the principal of a New Jersey high school remarked recently. "And all that girls think about," he added, "is driving the boys' cars." These statements may not be far from the truth. Almost every high school now has a driver-education class. Well, every high school should also have a buyer-education class, instructing youngsters in the various alternative ways of purchasing an automobile: Should one pay cash or finance the purchase? What are the relative merits of each method? What are the different ways of financing? Etc., etc.

The subject of how to finance one's college education can also provide practical training. What does college really cost, in terms of both education expenses and lost income while at school? What financial aid is available? What type of special loan funds and borrowing plans are available?

A course should teach just what a dollar is, what it can do, and the vital importance of saving. High-school girls should be instructed in how to purchase food and clothing, how to operate a household and how to provide for medical expenses and personal care.

The major thrust should be in high schools, but courses in the use of credit and the handling of family income should also be offered as part of community adult-education programs. The assistance of community organizations and labor groups should be sought in this regard.

Community debt-counseling programs do help in training people in the management of money, but their failure is that they concentrate their services on families who are in the gravest difficulty. The person in debt usually turns to the counseling service after he has exhausted every opportunity to borrow or negotiate payments with his creditors. One observer has characterized debt-counseling agencies as "financial first-aid stations that care for the wounded." No one can find fault with the work performed by a first-aid station. The problem is that there is nothing preventive about one. The number of counseling services could be tripled and it is not likely that the stream of financially crippled families would be checked to any marked degree.

The educational function of community counseling services could be broadened enormously. In some communities service staff members address high-school groups or community organizations. In a few cases counselors have appeared on local television programs. At best, these are quite modest achievements.

There are large loopholes in the country's credit-information and reporting system. Competing retailers or competing small-loan companies sometimes refuse to cooperate with local credit bureaus. There have been innumerable instances of credit records not being kept up to date, and thus a newly delinquent account may be described to a retailer as being in perfect order. The establishment of a central credit bureau in every trading area is one solution that has been proposed, but it is debatable whether this is practical.

By and large, however, the file of information provided by a local credit bureau is valid and up to date. By relying on it, a local retailer can reduce his credit losses and prevent people who are deep in debt from becoming completely engulfed by it. The problem is that more and more credit grantors will accept an account that is marginal or, worse, not even bother to run a credit check. More than one credit manager has been chastised because of too low a loss rate.

Credit managers must be criticized for the way in which they handle a newly delinquent account. Almost without exception they deal with these cases with a "wait and see" policy. It would be better to inquire why a customer has stopped paying or fails to pay and to offer financial counsel if debt trouble is apparent.

Research studies have shown clearly that the consumer, in all too many cases, simply won't or can't act in judicious fashion when it comes to credit buying. It is being left to the retailer to take the lead, to exercise greater selectivity in granting credit. The more responsible credit grantors are already exercising such restraint. One of the ironies of the situation is that should the nation's retailers and moneylenders fail to exercise more caution in their credit-extension policies, it is they who will be hurt the most.

Chapter XIII of the Bankruptcy Act can play a significant role in the rehabilitation of debt-burdened families. It enables a debtor to honor his obligations, and by so doing he retains his credit standing and preserves his self-respect. Straight bankruptcy, whether out of the country's onetime puritan ethic or the debtor's personal pride, is still regarded in a negative way in most areas. Chapter XIII is a practical alternative, but it is no panacea. Its use is advisable only in those cases where the repayment plan will not cause the debtor or his family unreasonable hardship. Where Chapter XIII has been put into effect, it has proved successful. But its use is terribly limited. The problem here seems to be one of informing and educating. Jacob Dim, referee in bankruptcy for the District of Minnesota, in recent testimony before a Senate subcommittee, declared, "We have been increasing them [Chapter XIII cases], and the one thing we don't have is the ability to disseminate an educational program to the public, so that they will know that such a type of thing exists. We need an educational program among the bar associations, so that they know such a program exists." This is part of the answer. An appalling number of attorneys, accountants and debtors are not even aware of the availability of Chapter XIII.

The Administrative Office of the United States Courts, the Consumer Bankruptcy Committee of the American Bar Association, the Judicial Conference of the United States, the National Bankruptcy Conference—all of these bodies have acted in recent years to improve the administration of Chapter XIII and encourage its use. But much of what has been done seems parochial in scope. Too few debtors, social agencies, lawyers and accountants are aware of Chapter XIII. A program to advise the public at large about this statute—what it is, how it functions and its benefits—is a necessity.

It might be helpful to rename this provision of the Bankruptcy Act. The term "Chapter XIII" is virtually meaningless to the lay person. Referee Dim has made the suggestion that the name of the bankruptcy court be changed to Court of Economic Rehabilitation. Somewhat the same type of name might be applied to Chapter XIII. "What bankruptcy courts really do," Referee Dim says, "they rehabilitate people [and] they rehabilitate businesses through chapter proceedings. . . ."

There can be no denying the fact that the incidence of bankruptcy bears a direct relationship to the harshness of state collection laws—that is, laws concerning attachment and garnishment. In many states people have a chilling fear of garnishment. They fear the drastic lowering of their wages, or the fact that their unsympathetic employer will fire them. Out of their fear they file bankruptcy.

There should be a national and uniform law concerning attachments and garnishments. They should not be abolished, as some legislators recommend. When no collection laws exist, credit losses are high. Instead, wage exemptions should be fixed at 85 to 90 percent for every state, with a minimum exemption high enough to allow the debtor to provide reasonable support for his family. These are suggestions put forth by Referee Lawrence Miller of the Northern District of Illinois. Legislation should also be enacted, as it has been in New York State, prohibiting an employer from firing a worker for wage garnishment.

Deficiency judgments, which in some states can be cruel and unfair, are another form of collection action that send debtors straight to bankruptcy court. A deficiency is the difference between what a buyer has agreed to pay for an item and what the seller gets for it after a repossession. Sometimes the debtor finds that he owes more on a deficiency judgment than he agreed to pay for the merchandise in the first place— and what really pains him is that he no longer has the merchandise.

One remedy here might be to allow the creditor either to repossess the merchandise or to sue for the balance due, but not both. Professor Vern Countryman, chairman of the Special Committee on Consumer Bankruptcy of the National Bankruptcy Conference, has proposed that the bankruptcy court, in Chapter XIII cases, be authorized to determine the value of the merchandise in question and to allow the deficiency claim only in the amount by which the indebtedness (plus the interest) exceeds the value.

One day uniformity in state collection laws may be a reality. The National Conference of Commissioners on Uniform State Laws, which is made up of representatives of each state, has drafted a uniform credit code. It covers not only collection but installment sales, consumer credit and small loans. Once a final draft has been approved by the conference, the code will be presented to each state legislature. This may be late in 1968 or in 1969. The approval of the various states, if it is to come, would take several additional years.

Uniformity should also be brought to the various state homestead and property exemptions. In California a bankrupt is allowed a $12,500 homestead exemption and personal property exemptions as well. But seven states and the District of Columbia have no homestead provisions at all. Most state exemptions statutes were obsolete generations ago. Today many are ludicrous.

Consumers—especially low-income consumers—need all the protection they can get when they venture into the market place, and federal legislation is required to give them that protection. The Truth-in-Lending and Truth-in-Packaging laws are mere beginnings. The establishment of a Department of Consumer Affairs, a measure proposed by Benjamin Rosenthal, a member of the House of Representatives from New York City, would be another step in the right direction. But such legislative efforts meet staunch and even arrogant opposition from business-oriented lobbies. They were successful in emasculating the Truth-in-Packaging law and their attacks on the Truth-in-Lending bill prevented that measure from coming to a vote in the Senate for an incredible seven years.

Some people have said that the rate of consumer bank-

ruptcies could be checked by setting a minimum amount on a
petitioner's indebtedness—say, $2,000. If a person owed
less than that, he would not be allowed to file. But such a law
could lead to some alarming abuses. With a $2,000 debt limit
in effect, a less than scrupulous lawyer might tell a client who
does not quite qualify to go out and run up some more bills
until he properly met conditions. Some people would not have
to be counseled to do this.

Periodically the suggestion is made to raise bankruptcy
courts to the level of district courts and to endow bankruptcy
referees with the status and authority of federal judges. In
1938, when the present system was developed, only a few
thousand bankruptcy cases were being heard each year and
there was little basis for establishing an independent bankruptcy court system. Now, with the total number of bankruptcy
cases approaching 250,000 annually, and with bankruptcy
becoming an increasingly important factor in the country's
economy, it is time for the bankruptcy court to throw off its
stepchild status.

While such a move would not have a direct bearing on the
problems expressed here, it would add to the administrative
efficiency of the court—and to a significant degree in some
instances. Referees do not have contempt power now; they
must refer such matters to U.S. district judges. They are not
empowered to empanel juries when a jury is necessary. They
cannot conduct proceedings under the provisions of Chapter X,
which has to do with the reorganization of businesses. The
recommended reform would give referees these powers. It
would also raise the dignity of the court in the eyes of the
public and the bar. This particular reform, as well as all
aspects of the Bankruptcy Act, are under study by a committee
appointed by the Supreme Court.

Since the founding of the United States, bankruptcy law

and administration have undergone profound change. But innovation and reform have always been precipitated by depression, panic and scandal. Hopefully the modifications now being expressed, in this chapter and elsewhere, can be instituted before crisis.

BIBLIOGRAPHY

Brosky, John J. *A Study of Personal Bankruptcy in the Seattle Metropolitan Area.* Seattle: Retail Credit Association of Seattle, 1965.

Brunner, George Allen. *Personal Bankruptcy: Trends and Characteristics.* Columbus, Ohio: Bureau of Business Research, College of Commerce and Administration, Ohio State University, 1965.

Caplovitz, David. *The Poor Pay More.* New York: The Free Press of Glencoe, 1963.

Cowans, Daniel R. *Bankruptcy Law and Practice.* St. Paul: West Publishing Co., 1963.

Dolphin, Robert, Jr. *An Analysis of Economic Factors and Personal Factors Leading to Consumer Bankruptcy.* East Lansing, Michigan: Graduate School of Business Administration, Michigan State University, 1965.

Earl, David. *The Bankruptians.* New York: Exposition Press, 1966.

Herrmann, Robert O. *Causal Factors in Consumer Bankruptcy: A Case Study.* Davis, California: Institute of Governmental Affairs, University of California, 1965.

Huber, Milton J. *A Study of Financially Over Extended Families.* Detroit: The Merrill-Palmer Institute, 1965.

Misbach, Grant L. *Personal Bankruptcy in the United States and Utah.* Salt Lake City: College of Business, University of Utah, 1964.

MacLachlan, James A. *Handbook of the Law of Bankruptcy.* St. Paul: West Publishing Co., 1956.

Twinem, Linn K. *Bankruptcy Guide for Consumer Finance Companies.* Beneficial Finance Co., 1964.

U.S. Government Printing Office, Washington, D. C., 1964. *Bankruptcy Laws of the United States,* Compiled by Gilman G. Udell.

Warren, Charles. *Bankruptcy in United States History.* Cambridge, Massachusetts: Harvard University Press, 1935.

Weintraub, Benjamin, and Levin, Harris. *Practical Guide to Bankruptcy and Debtor Relief.* Englewood Cliffs, New Jersey, Prentice-Hall, Inc., 1964.

GLOSSARY

ARRANGEMENT A financial settlement or adjustment.

ATTACHMENT The seizure by a creditor of property for which money is owed.

BANKRUPT A person who has filed a petition; a person who has been judged bankrupt—i.e., a person who has been legally declared unable to pay his debts.

BANKRUPTCY The filing of a formal petition and schedule in a United States District Court; the condition of being bankrupt.

CHANDLER ACT Amendments to the Bankruptcy Act enacted in 1938.

CHAPTER XIII A section of the Bankruptcy Act which provides that an insolvent wage earner may pay his debts out of his future earnings under court supervision.

CLERK The clerk of the court of bankruptcy.

COMPOSITION A settlement in which a debtor agrees to pay his creditors a portion of their claims.

CONSOLIDATION The combining of one's debts into a single debt, with the idea of paying a portion of the consolidated figure at regular intervals.

CONSUMER CREDIT An economic practice by virtue of which a person can obtain goods, services or cash for immediate use, repaying through future income over a short or intermediate period of time.

COURT The court of bankruptcy in which proceedings are pending or being heard.

CREDIT GRANTOR Any one of the usual sources which grant credit to the individual—banks, retail stores and consumer finance companies.

CREDIT INVESTIGATION An inquiry conducted by a credit grantor to determine whether a prospective customer merits credit.

CREDIT LOSS The money lost by a credit grantor when a debt is not paid.

CREDIT RATING An evaluation by a credit bureau and based, to a great extent, on an individual's past payment record, of his worthiness as a credit buyer.

CREDITOR Anyone who owns a demand or claim.

199

DEBT   Any obligation, liability, demand or claim.

DEBTOR   One who owes debts; the petitioner in a Chapter XIII filing.

DEFICIENCY JUDGMENT   A judgment obtained by a creditor following the sale of a debtor's property (an automobile, for instance) in the amount of the balance owed on the property.

DELINQUENT   A credit account which is past due.

DISCHARGE   The release of the bankrupt from all provable debts, excluding those exempted by the Bankruptcy Act.

DISCRETIONARY INCOME   The amount remaining from one's take-home pay after essential living costs have been met.

DISTRICT   One of the United States Federal Districts in the courts of which a bankruptcy petition may be filed.

DURABLE GOODS   Those commodities which are useful to a consumer over an extended period of time—i.e., an automobile, appliances, furniture.

EXECUTION   A writ, issued by a court, giving authority to put a judgment in effect; a validation of any legal instrument.

EXEMPTION   That portion of a person's wage not subject to garnishment; also, those assets which under state law are immune to the claim of a bankruptcy court.

EXTENSION   An additional period of time allowed a debtor in making payment.

GARNISH   To bring garnishment proceedings; to garnishee.

GARNISHMENT   A legal notice to an employer which directs him to withhold a portion of the debtor's wages in satisfaction of a creditor's claim.

INSOLVENT   The condition of not being able to pay one's debts; an insolvent person.

INVOLUNTARY PETITION   A condition of bankruptcy forced by one's creditors who seek an equal distribution of the bankrupt's property and the forestallment of his discharge.

JUDGMENT   A debt substantiated by a court order which paves the way for garnishment or attachment.

LIEN   A creditor's claim on the property of a debtor as security against the payment of a debt.

LIQUIDATION   To settle debts by selling one's property and apportioning the money received to the creditors.

PETITION   A request filed in a court of bankruptcy "praying" for the benefits of the Bankruptcy Act.

PETITIONER   One who files a petition. In straight bankruptcy proceedings, the petitioner is regarded as a bankrupt; in Chapter XIII cases, the petitioner is considered a debtor.

PRORATER   An individual or firm which, for a monthly fee or percentage charge, receives a family's funds and distributes them to creditors; also called a debt pooler, debt consolidator.

RECEIVER   A person approved by the court to administer or hold in
trust property in bankruptcy.

REFEREE   The person appointed in a bankruptcy case to take testimony, study the proceedings and report his judgment.

REFINANCE   To renegotiate and revise the payment schedule of an
existing debt.

REPOSSESS   To reclaim a piece of property (usually durable goods)
which has been purchased through an installment sales contract
and for which payment is past due.

SECURED CREDITOR   A creditor who has security for his debt on the
property or assets of the bankrupt.

SHORT- AND INTERMEDIATE-TERM CREDIT   Debt which is repaid over a
relatively short span of time.

STATEMENT OF AFFAIRS   Information filed with the bankruptcy court
by the petitioner that relates to his assets and liabilities.

STRAIGHT BANKRUPTCY   A voluntary filing in which the petitioner
seeks a discharge of his debts; opposed to an involuntary bankruptcy proceeding or a Chapter XIII filing.

TRUSTEE   In a bankruptcy proceeding, the person into whose hands
the property of the petitioner is delivered; the elected or court-
appointed representative of the creditors.

VOLUNTARY BANKRUPTCY   A bankruptcy filing of one's free choice;
distinguished from an involuntary filing.

WAGE EARNER   An individual who works for salary, wages or hire.

WAGE-EARNER PLAN   See Chapter XIII.

APPENDIX

Statistics

The statistics that follow were provided by the Research Services Division of the National Consumer Finance Association and are based on information supplied by the Administrative Office of the United States Courts, Washington, D.C.

The number of filings for each year refer to the number of proceedings commenced.

"Non-business" filings are those listed in the federal source as "employee" and "others not in business." Puerto Rico, the Virgin Islands and Guam are not included.

TABLE I
Non-Business Bankruptcy Proceedings

	1957*	1962	1964	1965	1966	1967
Alabama	8,393	9,224	9,799	9,744	9,434	10,095
Alaska	4	30	57	81	117	129
Arizona	379	2,044	3,092	3,103	3,256	3,350
Arkansas	172	371	433	556	693	777
California	9,899	23,723	26,980	30,197	34,255	36,996
Colorado	1,406	2,340	3,344	3,777	3,830	4,358
Connecticut	456	856	1,132	1,133	1,138	1,344
Delaware	17	48	46	51	58	56
District of Columbia	76	96	78	66	68	64
Florida	87	388	525	589	863	1,126
Georgia	2,185	5,949	7,362	7,815	7,481	7,382
Hawaii	89	170	239	299	337	384

* Fiscal years ending June 30.

Idaho	241	634	740	780	836	942
Illinois	7,658	13,705	14,900	13,587	13,829	13,452
Indiana	673	3,636	4,984	5,420	5,892	6,754
Iowa	331	1,452	1,657	1,559	1,601	1,899
Kansas	1,216	2,766	2,770	2,764	3,168	3,261
Kentucky	1,380	2,624	3,521	3,908	4,256	4,794
Louisiana	503	1,772	2,505	2,473	2,368	2,790
Maine	643	1,519	1,760	1,577	1,554	1,791
Maryland	52	169	183	203	242	267
Massachusetts	647	840	1,082	1,120	1,254	1,443
Michigan	2,587	6,089	5,585	6,009	6,628	8,055
Minnesota	1,372	2,738	2,817	2,899	3,251	3,394
Mississippi	95	420	781	878	1,011	1,037
Missouri	1,185	3,214	4,449	4,490	5,059	5,422
Montana	150	504	392	521	549	618
Nebraska	343	609	951	878	984	1,144
Nevada	70	358	572	816	990	1,298
New Hampshire	72	372	619	728	756	836
New Jersey	255	751	811	886	1,025	1,220
New Mexico	104	510	866	962	933	1,035
New York	2,193	3,963	5,033	5,549	6,153	6,589
North Carolina	15	58	109	157	204	271
North Dakota	33	123	168	190	220	219
Ohio	5,218	13,039	14,647	15,838	16,979	18,497
Oklahoma	819	1,767	2,626	2,771	3,327	3,845
Oregon	1,926	3,605	3,671	3,909	4,400	4,860
Pennsylvania	139	512	624	636	708	1,010
Rhode Island	206	240	353	361	436	510
South Carolina	4	79	97	165	128	118
South Dakota	30	79	113	159	141	171
Tennessee	3,559	6,654	8,507	8,812	9,470	10,052
Texas	43	235	259	395	426	551
Utah	413	620	1,171	1,191	1,337	1,557
Vermont	75	162	260	281	325	319
Virginia	1,991	3,618	4,129	4,288	4,431	4,984
Washington	1,990	3,070	3,686	3,892	4,280	4,688
West Virginia	714	1,210	1,302	1,391	1,453	1,625
Wisconsin	1,424	2,894	3,028	3,122	3,344	3,936
Wyoming	69	259	367	420	423	394
TOTAL	63,601	132,117	155,182	163,396	175,901	191,709

TABLE II

Increase or Decrease in Number of Non-Business Bankruptcies
(Per 100,000 Population)

	INCREASE OR DECREASE IN NUMBER OF BANKRUPTCIES				NUMBER OF BANKRUPTCIES PER 100,000 POPULATION**			
	1957* to 1962	1962 to 1967	1966 over 1965	1967 over 1966	1957	1962	1966	19
Alabama	831	871	–310	661	273	277	271	2
Alaska	26	99	36	12	2	13	44	
Arizona	1,665	1,306	153	94	36	145	207	2
Arkansas	199	406	137	84	10	20	36	
California	13,833	13,264	4,058	2,741	72	144	186	1
Colorado	934	2,018	53	528	87	128	197	2
Connecticut	400	488	5	206	20	33	40	
Delaware	31	8	7	–2	4	10	12	
District of Columbia	20	–32	2	–4	10	12	8	
Florida	301	738	274	263	2	7	15	
Georgia	3,764	1,433	–334	–99	59	148	170	1
Hawaii	81	214	38	47	16	26	47	
Idaho	393	308	56	106	38	92	121	1
Illinois	6,047	–253	242	–377	80	135	130	1
Indiana	2,963	3,118	472	862	15	77	120	1
Iowa	1,121	447	42	298	12	53	58	
Kansas	1,550	495	404	93	57	124	141	1
Kentucky	1,244	2,170	348	538	48	85	134	1
Louisiana	1,269	1,018	–105	422	17	54	67	
Maine	876	272	–23	237	69	153	158	1
Maryland	117	98	39	25	2	5	7	
Massachusetts	193	603	134	189	13	16	23	
Michigan	3,502	1,966	619	1,427	35	77	80	
Minnesota	1,366	656	352	143	42	79	91	

* See note to Table I.
** Population as of beginning of respective fiscal year.
*** Less than 1 bankruptcy per 100,000 population.

	INCREASE OR DECREASE IN NUMBER OF BANKRUPTCIES				NUMBER OF BANKRUPTCIES PER 100,000 POPULATION**			
	1957* to 1962	1962 to 1967	1966 over 1965	1967 over 1966	1957	1962	1966	1967
ississippi	325	617	133	26	5	19	44	44
issouri	2,029	2,208	569	363	28	74	113	119
ontana	354	114	28	69	23	73	78	88
braska	266	535	106	160	25	42	67	79
vada	288	940	174	308	28	115	228	301
w Hampshire	300	464	28	80	13	60	112	123
w Jersey	496	469	139	195	5	12	15	18
w Mexico	406	525	−29	102	13	53	92	103
w York	1,770	2,626	604	436	14	23	34	36
orth Carolina	43	213	47	67	***	1	4	5
orth Dakota	90	96	30	−1	5	19	34	34
io	7,821	5,458	1,141	1,518	57	132	166	178
lahoma	948	2,078	556	518	36	74	136	155
egon	1,679	1,255	491	460	113	202	227	246
nnsylvania	373	498	72	302	1	4	6	9
ode Island	34	270	75	74	25	28	49	57
uth Carolina	75	39	−37	−10	***	3	5	5
uth Dakota	49	92	−18	30	4	11	21	25
nnessee	3,095	3,398	658	582	104	183	246	260
xas	192	316	31	125	***	2	4	5
ah	207	937	146	220	51	66	135	155
rmont	87	157	44	−6	20	42	80	78
rginia	1,627	1,366	143	553	53	88	100	112
ashington	1,080	1,618	388	408	75	106	144	154
est Virginia	496	415	62	172	38	66	80	90
isconsin	1,470	1,042	222	592	38	73	81	94
yoming	190	135	3	−29	22	77	128	124
OTAL	68,516	59,592	12,505	15,808	38	72	91	98

TABLE III
Chapter XIII Filings

	CHAPTER XIII PROCEEDINGS COMMENCED				CHAPTER XIII PROCEEDINGS AS A % OF ALL NON-BUSINE BANKRUPTCY PROCEEDINGS			
	1957*	1962	1966	1967	1957	1962	1966	1967
Alabama	7,454	7,952	7,438	8,019	89	86	79	79
Alaska	—	4	7	—	—	13	6	—
Arizona	2	149	177	166	1	7	5	5
Arkansas	123	227	462	445	72	61	67	57
California	103	1,937	3,482	4,356	1	8	10	12
Colorado	—	50	468	580	—	2	12	13
Connecticut	—	21	14	14	—	2	1	1
Delaware	1	2	—	1	6	4	—	2
District of Columbia	—	5	6	10	—	5	9	16
Florida	—	42	33	29	—	11	4	3
Georgia	618	1,950	2,691	2,477	28	33	36	34
Hawaii	1	30	52	72	1	18	15	19
Idaho	62	94	131	148	26	15	16	16
Illinois	65	664	691	886	1	5	5	7
Indiana	25	95	44	57	4	3	1	1
Iowa	129	317	180	194	39	22	11	10
Kansas	643	1,622	1,321	1,355	53	59	42	42
Kentucky	99	202	930	1,123	7	8	22	23
Louisiana	1	26	96	110	—	1	4	4
Maine	168	757	765	895	26	50	49	50
Maryland	1	16	5	2	2	9	2	1
Massachusetts	2	14	25	27	—	2	2	2
Michigan	10	119	454	801	—	2	7	10
Minnesota	5	694	609	588	—	25	19	17
Mississippi	6	86	42	32	6	20	4	3
Missouri	443	263	192	252	37	8	4	5
Montana	2	19	5	11	1	4	1	2
Nebraska	—	38	71	63	—	6	7	6
Nevada	—	9	23	37	—	3	2	3
New Hampshire	1	10	—	—	1	3	—	—

* See note to Table I.

	CHAPTER XIII PROCEEDINGS COMMENCED				CHAPTER XIII PROCEEDINGS AS A % OF ALL NON-BUSINESS BANKRUPTCY PROCEEDINGS			
	1957	1962	1966	1967	1957	1962	1966	1967
w Jersey	—	154	122	139	—	21	12	11
w Mexico	2	122	167	145	2	24	18	14
w York	18	94	39	42	1	2	1	1
rth Carolina	—	18	58	113	—	31	28	42
rth Dakota	—	5	3	7	—	4	1	3
io	1	373	1,360	1,881	—	3	8	10
lahoma	1	33	66	67	—	2	2	2
egon	8	113	110	269	—	3	3	6
nnsylvania	—	31	22	11	—	6	3	1
ode Island	—	5	4	4	—	2	1	1
uth Carolina	—	22	15	10	—	28	12	8
uth Dakota	—	8	4	1	—	10	3	1
nnessee	1,431	3,252	4,130	4,397	40	49	44	44
xas	—	33	22	61	—	14	5	11
ah	—	30	59	108	—	5	4	7
rmont	—	—	3	—	—	—	1	—
rginia	77	452	704	774	4	12	16	16
shington	2	337	556	690	—	11	13	15
st Virginia	18	68	47	56	3	6	3	3
sconsin	26	314	354	429	2	11	11	11
yoming	1	2	2	2	1	1	—	1
TAL	11,549	22,880	28,261	31,956	18	17	16	17

INDEX